Other books by Mark Brackenbury

Begin Cruising Under Sail published by Elliot Right Way Books
Norwegian Cruising Guide published by Stanford Maritime
Frisian Pilot published by Stanford Maritime
Scottish West Coast Pilot published by Stanford Maritime
Baltic Southwest Pilot published by Stanford Maritime

Normandy and Channel Islands Pilot
Calais to St Malo
The Seine to Rouen
The Channel Islands

Mark Brackenbury

Based on the original work *Normandy Harbours and Pilotage* by Edward Delmar-Morgan

ADLARD COLES LIMITED
GRANADA PUBLISHING
London Toronto Sydney New York

Published by Granada Publishing in
Adlard Coles Limited, 1983

First published as
Normandy Harbours and Pilotage by Edward Delmar-Morgan, 1969
Second Edition 1973
Third edition revised by Mark Brackenbury 1978
Fourth edition revised by Mark Brackenbury 1980

Fifth edition as
Normandy and Channel Islands Pilot by Mark Brackenbury 1983

Granada Publishing Limited
Frogmore, St Albans, Herts, AL2 2NF
and
36 Golden Square, London W1R 4AH
515 Madison Avenue, New York, NY 10022, USA
60 International Boulevard, Rexdale, Ontario, R9W 6J2, Canada
61 Beach Road, Auckland, New Zealand

Copyright © Mark Brackenbury 1983

ISBN 0 229 11697 3

Filmset and printed in Great Britain by
BAS Printers Limited, Over Wallop, Hampshire

Granada ®
Granada Publishing ®

Contents

List of Charts and Diagrams

Introduction

This book is based on the original *Normandy Harbours and Pilotage* by Edward Delmar-Morgan, first published in 1969. Sadly, he died shortly after completing a major revision of the book in 1973, and when it became clear that developments and changes along the coast had made much of the information in that edition out of date, the publishers, Adlard Coles Ltd, did me the honour of asking me to make a further major revision in 1978. This was followed by a further revision in 1980.

When the time came in 1982 for yet another edition to be prepared for publication in 1983, it was decided that it would be sensible to extend the coverage to include the west coast of the Cotentin peninsula as far as St Malo, also taking in the fascinating and complex cruising area of the Channel Islands. By this time, so great had the changes been along the coastline originally covered, that very little could remain of the information assembled by Edward Delmar-Morgan, apart from the historical notes about the various ports he covered. So, taking all these factors into account, it was decided that the time had come to allow Edward's name to retire from the title page: I would, however, like to express here the great debt I owe him for constructing the original framework of the book.

The object of the extension of coverage was to fill in the important gap that previously existed between the old *Normandy Harbours and Pilotage* and the same publishers' *North Brittany Pilot*: the Adlard Coles Ltd pilotage series now covers the European mainland coast unbrokenly from Den Helder in Holland to La Coruña in Spain.

I have always been a great believer in the vital importance of regular personal visits to all the harbours in any area for which I am providing pilotage information, and I was fortunate enough to be able to revisit virtually every harbour mentioned in this book during the 1982 season. With the pace of development now visibly slowing, I think it may be hoped that the bulk of the information contained in this latest edition may remain accurate for some years ahead, although there will inevitably be some further changes and developments.

The coasts from Calais to Cherbourg, the span of the original book, may not have the spectacular beauty of the north Brittany coast, but they have great charm, and many British yachtsmen become positive addicts. Cruising the area presents no particular difficulties to the experienced navigator, although there are stretches where there is no good refuge in heavy onshore weather, so it is important to pay due heed to weather forecasts and other factors. The stretch of over fifty miles between Boulogne and Dieppe is perhaps the one that needs to be watched most carefully: none of the intervening harbours can safely be entered in a westerly gale, which makes it a long and inhospitable stretch in such conditions.

To the west of Cherbourg, including the Channel Islands, lie waters with a rocky, rugged beauty more like the Brittany coasts, and with their own especial interest and excitement arising from the great tidal range and the powerful streams that are therefore encountered in that area. It is hoped that the particular attention that has been given to passage notes and approaches in the section of the book covering this tricky area will be of help to newcomers planning their first passages through these fascinating but undeniably tricky channels. General notes on cruising in the Channel Islands will be found at the beginning of the section of the book covering them.

Altogether the book now covers an enchanting and so far surprisingly uncrowded cruising area, conveniently placed for owners whose boats are berthed on either the east or south coasts of England, and one in which I for one have spent many happy summers. I hope the reader will find the material contained herein useful: if any errors or changes are detected, please do not hesitate to write to me care of the Publishers.

Charts, Tide Tables Etc.

A tremendous choice of charts is available to cover this region: apart from the British Admiralty charts (excellent, but without port plans for the most part) there are charts from the French Admiralty, yachtsmens' charts produced by Imray, Laurie, Norie, and Wilson and by Stanford Maritime in England, and various French equivalents of which the most popular is probably the Carte Guide Navigation Cotiere series, to be found on sale in almost all French chandlers. Be warned, however, that these are dated very inconspicuously (on the lower right back cover), and are often left on sale two or three years after printing, with no corrections. I also personally find their brightly coloured pictorial style rather difficult to use, but some of my friends swear by them.

Information about tidal ranges and the speed and direction of offshore streams is given at the end of almost every port section, but one important point must be made. The time differences given in the invaluable Reed's Almanac are based on mean tides, and the actual time difference between the standard port and the subsidiary one being studied can vary from the Reed's figure by as much as twenty minutes at extreme springs or neaps. These times can be critical when cruising in this area, as they determine the opening times of the dock gates, and indeed the time when one may safely approach or leave the many harbours with drying approaches, so readers will be very well advised to use the full Admiralty Tide Tables, or the French equivalent, from which differences can be calculated at all heights of tide.

The area from Calais to Cherbourg is adequately covered in my view by Admiralty charts 2451, 2612 and 2613, together with 1106 if the smaller ports or inshore passages of North Cotentin are contemplated. To get the full pleasure of cruising in the Channel Islands, I do not think the commercial charts are adequate, though they allow visits to the major ports.

For 'rock-hopping' short cuts and the use of the minor harbours and anchorages, the large scale Admiralty charts must be carried. I would suggest as a minimum No 2669 (or the Imray or Stanford equivalents) as a passage chart, together with No 60 for Alderney and Burhou, 808 for E Guernsey, Herm and Sark, 3655 for Jersey, 3659 for the coast around St Malo, and 2700 for the approaches to that port. One or two other charts are mentioned in the text for special places, but the above will provide good general cover of the area for normal purposes.

Finally, a word about the title. It would be difficult to find an equally descriptive title that was not unduly cumbersome, but it should be recorded that Normandy in fact only starts with the SW pier at Le Tréport. The NE pier and parts north are in Picardy.

Mark Brackenbury
September 1982

Pilotage: Calais to Fécamp

Charts Nos. 1892, 2451, 2612, 2613

Both in reaching Calais or Boulogne from England, and in the northern part of the coast covered by this book, the main problem is a man-made one: the traffic separation scheme in the Dover Straits. Crossing the lanes must be done as nearly as possible at right angles, and when proceeding down the coast great care must be taken not to stand so far out to sea as to wander into the NE-going lane, which is only 2·6 miles offshore at its nearest. The lanes are clearly shown on Admiralty Chart No. 1892.

Shoals extend nearly two miles offshore between Caps Blanc-Nez and Gris-Nez, so it is advisable to pass north of the IALA starboard buoys CA3 (Fl. G. 4 s.) and CA1: the latter is unlit, so at night substitute the W Cardinal buoy a mile to the W, lit VQ (9) 10s. From here or CA1, a course can safely be laid to pass a mile W of Cap Gris-Nez, after which keep at least that offing until Boulogne pierhead towers or lights are seen, when they can be steered for.

South of Boulogne the separation zone is soon far offshore, and the only dangers more than a mile offshore are the sandbanks which bulge seawards from the estuaries of the Canche, Authie and Somme. In poor visibility these areas can be tricky, and the careful navigator should keep a good offing while passing each bay, and only close with the coast again when he is sure that he has passed them.

SW of Le Tréport the few hazards are never more than $\frac{1}{2}$ mile offshore, apart from the 1 m wreck NNW of Pte d'Ailly, marked by a N cardinal buoy, VQ. Either pass north of this, or *at least* $\frac{1}{2}$ mile to the south.

It is worth making the point that along the part of the coast that consists of cliffs (i.e. from Le Tréport to Fécamp) the harbours and coastal towns all lie in natural breaks in the cliff line. This has two effects: one is that they all look very similar and are difficult to tell apart, the other that they are often invisible from a boat sailing fairly close in along the coast until they are nearly abeam. It can be quite disconcerting to see a line of apparently unbroken cliffs stretching ahead for miles when your destination is a harbour that the chart says is only a couple of miles ahead, but if your navigation is right it will turn up on cue, appearing like magic out of an apparently smooth cliff.

Calais

Charts Nos. 1892, 1352

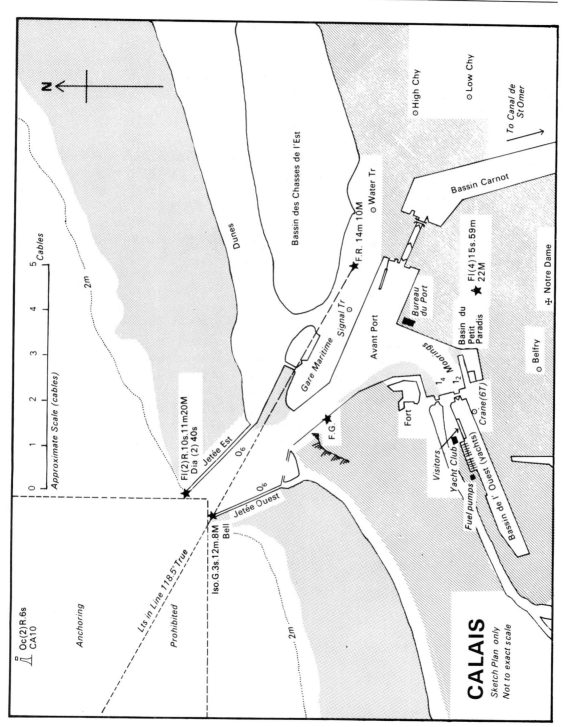

Plan 1   Calais

Calais has been associated with maritime England from time immemorial and indeed it was the last English possession on the French mainland to be lost. There is little doubt now that foreign yachtsmen can consider Calais as an excellent port to visit: good shopping facilities and absolute safety in the yacht harbour, both from the elements and from petty thieving, are amongst its attractions. Furthermore, access and approaches are relatively easy.

Approaches
The harbour entrance to Calais faces roughly NW and there is no difficulty when within half-a-mile. But about a mile N of the entrance Ridens de la Rade, a sandbank which is long and narrow and which shoals at one place to 0·3 metres is a hazard—in bad weather seas break heavily upon it.

Approach from the E
Although a deep water passage between the sandbank and the shore does exist, it is narrow and unmarked. It is therefore necessary to pass outside the Ridens until the shallowest part has been cleared. The shore should be given a berth of at least two miles until the pierheads bear south, when it is safe to alter course for them, but checking constantly to make sure that any eastgoing tide is counteracted. In calm weather and at half-tide or above, these precautions are of course unnecessary. Conversely, in strong onshore winds, it is wise to hold a course parallel to the shore until buoy CA6 (Oc R4s) can be identified and left to port, as the sea can break heavily on the deeper western part of the shoal, even though there is a depth of $3\frac{1}{2}$ metres at L.A.T. At night, remember that the main Calais light (Fl. (4) 15 s), lies nearly a mile to the east of the pierheads, so from the east, course should not be altered until the bearing has decreased to 160° (mag.).

Approach from the W
The red buoys CA8 and CA10 should be left to port and a new course for the harbour entrance should not be made until CA10 is nearly abeam. A glance at Chart No. 1892 will show the configurations quite clearly.

1. Calais: the harbour entrance.

In addition to the foregoing instructions, it is important to allow for the strong tidal stream which sets across the entrance. If arrival has been timed for high water, to allow speedy entry to the inner harbour, the rate can be as much as 3 knots ENEly at springs. As well as the cross-set, strong swirls may be encountered, so the piers should be given a wide berth.

In daytime a simple rule is to keep the lighthouse on the end of the western breakwater in line with the tall chimney (easily visible) when the tide is running to the east. When the tide is running to the west keep the lighthouse on the end of the eastern breakwater in line with the main Calais lighthouse. Traffic signals (shown from the Gare Maritime) are not

2. Calais: Avant Port, southern limb.

mandatory on yachts, but ferry traffic is exceptionally heavy and boats equipped with VHF are advised to clear entry and departure with Port Control on Channel 12. In any event a good lookout must be kept for vessels entering or leaving, and yachts must keep well over to their starboard side.

After entering the harbour between the two breakwaters proceed straight ahead to the Avant Port which then divides: these two limbs are at right-angles to each other, the Avant Port de l'Est and the Avant Port de l'Ouest. The eastern limb takes the cross-channel

9

ferries on the northern side and fishing vessels on the southern side. Yachts should not try to moor anywhere in the Avant Port de l'Est but should turn to starboard into the Avant Port de l'Ouest. (It may be noted, however, that the continuation of the Avant Port de l'Est communicates by means of two parallel locks with a basin for small craft, forming the termination of the Canal de Calais, a route to Terneuzen and intermediate ports.) The east wall of the Avant Port de l'Ouest near the harbour office is quite suitable to lie against as a temporary measure, but only for two-thirds of its length. The southernmost third dries, as does the Bassin du Petit Paradis which opens immediately to the south-west. Owners of bilge keelers should

3. Calais: entrance to the yacht harbour.

resist any temptation to moor alongside the southern part and dry out, as the bottom is dangerous (1982) with jagged rocks and other obstructions. There is a grid in the Bassin du Petit Paradis which may be available for use: inspect it at low water before using. The harbourmaster will advise and make the necessary arrangements.

Most yachts can normally take advantage of the mooring buoys laid outside the lock gates, but it must be stressed that in the whole of the Avant Port, even in calm weather, there is a nasty scend, very often enough to make those with queasy stomachs feel seasick (just like Dover). There are 28 of these mooring buoys, which are intended for yachtsmen waiting for the dock gates to open, or for vessels that have left the Port de Plaisance at high tide, but wish to wait before leaving the port. There is a rule that no buoy may be occupied for more than one tide, but even so, on busy days and particularly at weekends it is often impossible to find a free buoy during the last hour or two before the gates and bridge open, and it is then necessary to moor against the quay wall. The dock gates open $2\frac{1}{2}$ hours before HW, and close 1 hour after or later; approximate bridge opening times are HW $-2\frac{1}{2}$, -1 and $+1$ on weekdays, $-2\frac{1}{2}$, $-\frac{1}{2}$ and $+1\frac{1}{2}$ at weekends. Exact times are posted at the control building at the S end of the bridge. Light signals at the bridge: Amber—bridge will open in ten minutes; Green—pass through; Red—do not pass through. Once in the basin, visitors berth alongside the long pontoon on the starboard side, except boats over 12 metres LOA, who lie alongside the south wall of the basin.

4. Calais: Port de Plaisance. Visitors moorings and clubhouse (with tricolors over it). Reproduced with the permission of the *Chambre de Commerce et d'Industrie de Calais*.

The yacht club (YC du Nord de la France) is large and friendly, with excellent shower and toilet facilities as well as a pleasant bar overlooking the basin. Its telephone number is (21) 34-55-23. Harbour dues, which are moderate for the facilities, are collected by M. Henri Bessodes, harbourmaster of the yacht harbour. His office is on the ground floor of the yacht club, but he is usually on the pontoon for daytime bridge openings to advise on berthing.

Duty-free stores are readily available through the club, on any day except Sunday. Customs office in the Rue Lamy. Tel: (21) 34-75-40. Strangely enough for such a popular harbour there is no chandler, nor repair facilities. Fuel in yacht basin (see Plan 1). Excellent shopping near the yacht basin, and many good restaurants at all price levels.

Tidal information
HEIGHT ABOVE DATUM OF SOUNDINGS IN METRES

High water		Low water	
Mean springs	Mean neaps	Mean springs	Mean neaps
6·9	5·6	0·7	1·8

The ENE stream starts at HW Dover $- 1\frac{3}{4}$, and reaches a peak of 2.9 knots (mean springs) at HW Dover. The WSW stream starts at HW Dover $+ 4\frac{1}{2}$, and reaches a peak of 2.5 knots (mean springs) at $- 5$.

Boulogne

Charts Nos. 1892 and 438

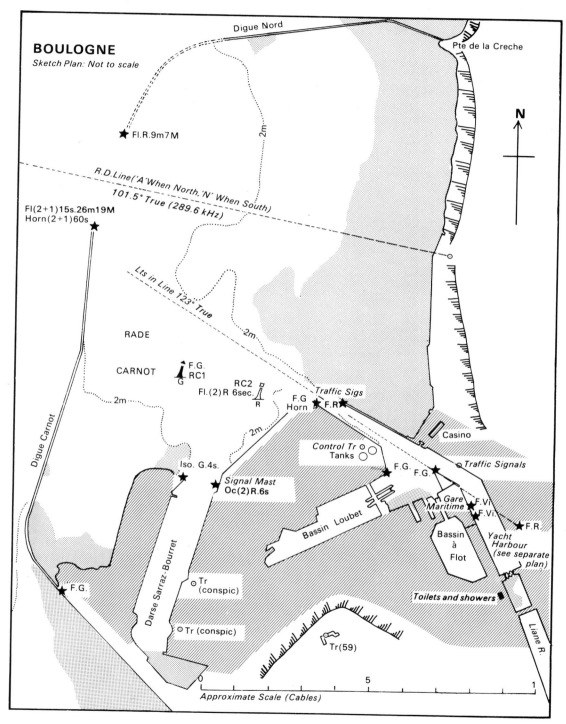

BOULOGNE
Sketch Plan: Not to scale

Digue Nord

Pte de la Creche

Fl.R.9m7M

R.D.Line ('A' When North, 'N' When South)
101.5° True (289.6 kHz)

N

Fl(2+1)15s.26m19M
Horn(2+1)60s

Lts in Line 123° True

2m

RADE

CARNOT

F.G.
RC1

RC2
Fl.(2)R 6sec.

Traffic Sigs

F.G
Horn   F.R

Casino

2m

Digue Carnot

2m

Iso. G.4s.

Signal Mast
Oc(2)R.6s

Control Tr
Tanks

F.G. F.G.

Traffic Signals

Gare
Maritime

F.Vi.
F.Vi.

F.R.

Bassin Loubet

Bassin
à
Flot

Yacht
Harbour
(see separate
plan)

F.G.

Darse Sarraz-Bourret

Tr
(conspic)

Tr (conspic)

Toilets and showers

Tr(59)

Liane R.

0   5   1
Approximate Scale (Cables)

Plan 2   Boulogne.

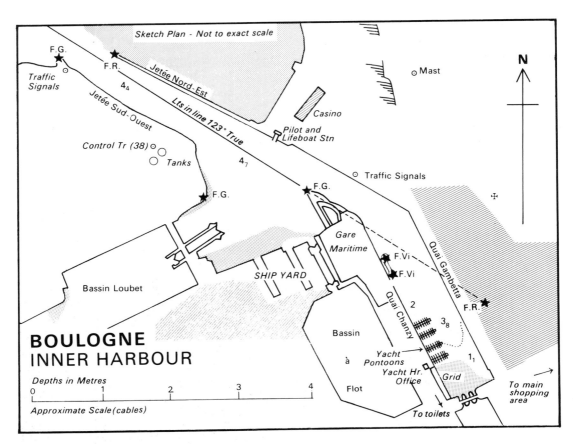

Plan 3 Boulogne, Inner Harbour.

14

Ever since proper facilities for yachts were first introduced, Boulogne has been one of the most popular ports on the north coast of France, owing to its commanding position as a point of departure for the south and east coasts of England, or as a starting point for cruises along the Normandy coast or further afield. It is an excellent, safe and comfortable harbour, available in all weathers, and with the additional advantage that shelter and a temporary mooring are available at any state of the tide. Unfortunately its popularity leads to overcrowding during the season, while there has been sadly little expenditure on upkeep and maintenance in recent years, with the result that the pontoons are in poor condition, and several mooring bollards damaged and unreliable in strong winds.

5. Boulogne: masthead view of the entrance to the outer harbour.

Identification

It is perhaps less difficult to identify Boulogne than many other ports along this coast; it is so large and there is a great deal of traffic in and out. Naturally, since the harbour is in a dip of the surrounding hills there is sometimes mist or fog obscuring the town itself.

If approaching in bad visibility, there is a directional radio beacon which leads directly into the harbour on a bearing of $101\frac{1}{2}°$ (T). It transmits on 289.6 kHz: 'A' (·–) when north of the line, 'N' (–·) when south of it, and a continuous note when on it. It has a range of five miles. Approaching from further off, the new radio beacon on the Cap d'Alprech light, which has a range of 20 miles, it will be found useful. It transmits 'PH' (· — — · ····) on 310·3 kHz at 03, 09 etc.

The most noticeable features to be seen on the hills behind Boulogne are the cathedral, a tall column to the north of the town (La Colonne de la Grande-Armée), and a square watchtower to the S.

Entrance

The entrance to Boulogne is $\frac{1}{4}$ mile wide and presents no difficulties, although it can be very rough in onshore gales. Until inside, allowance must be made for the tidal stream which can exceed 2 knots.

A feature of the entrance to the outer harbour is that the southern limb ends in a fairly large concrete structure with a lighthouse (white with a black top), but the northern limb does not join up with the port hand lighthouse (on an openwork concrete structure). There is a sunken groyne joining the two; this dries out at the landward end and it is inadvisable to attempt to cross it.

6. Boulogne: entrance to the inner harbour showing signalling station on southern pierhead and, to the right, the observation and control tower. Keep close along the mole on the left of the picture, to reach the yacht harbour.

Approach to yacht harbour

Immediately upon entering the outer harbour, course should be changed to 170° (mag.) for about half-a-mile to avoid shallow ground to the E. Once the S side of the N inner mole can be seen, or at night when the light structure at the Gare Maritime (fixed green) is in line with the light tower (fixed red located on top of the last but one of 5 blocks of flats) bearing 123° (True), the entrance is simple. Proceed straight down between the two moles, keeping a course parallel to the NE mole and at the end of the Quai Gambetta the pontoons will be seen on the starboard hand. When entering the inner harbour, traffic signals may be ignored as long as one proceeds with caution, *except* if Green above White above Red is shown from the signal tower. This is 'La Grande Interdiction', prohibiting all movement in the inner harbour, and must be obeyed by vessels of any kind whatever.

16

Berthing

Visiting yachts are accommodated alongside the pontoon that runs along the quay, *between* the projecting pontoons with 'box' berths. However, deep draft yachts may ground here at springs, as there is $1\frac{1}{2}$ m less water than at the outside ends, which have about 2·4 m at LWS. The harbour master may allot a box berth if asked; or moor outside the end of a pontoon. On no account go beyond the line of the most southerly pontoon, as the bottom shelves sharply with rocks. Boats over 40 ft moor to the wall below the Gare Maritime. Dues (1982) are high.

Facilities

There is a grid on the far end of the Quai Chanzy, opposite the rocks just referred to: it is under the supervision of the Chamber of Commerce, on the Quai Gambetta, where enquiries for use should be made. The grid is 6–7 ft from the wall: have a good look at low water. The position of bearers is marked in yellow paint on the wall above.

7. Boulogne: yacht moorings and grid on the Quai Chanzy.

On the Boulevard Gambetta (behind the Quai) is a row of bistros, cafés and small restaurants; and others of all prices and standards can be found in the main town, and also in the walled city on the hill above, which is well worth a visit.

There is a small yacht club at 236 Bde de St Beuve, 250 m past the Casino, but it is mainly dinghy oriented, and mostly used at weekends. Water available from a hose on the pontoons: fuel is now only available in cans from the Fina garage on the Quai Gambetta. The Capitainerie office is near the top of the access ramp, and is open 0700–2100. The duty-free suppliers (order-forms available at Capitainerie) are closed after 1200 on Saturday and all Sunday. Charts

(French) from Librairie Ranson, 50 rue de la Lampe, which runs up towards town from the bridge beyond the one at the top of the yacht harbour. Good toilets and showers are available for visitors in a building on the W side of the motor-boat harbour, the basin immediately SSW of the yacht harbour. These facilities are at the north end of the building, most of which serves as waiting rooms for ferry and hovercraft services. The doors are kept locked: key from the Capitainerie. Customs 3 bde Daumou, Tel. (21) 30-14-24.

Tidal information

HEIGHT ABOVE DATUM OF SOUNDINGS IN METRES

High Water		Low Water	
Mean springs	Mean neaps	Mean springs	Mean neaps
8·9	7·1	0·8	2·6

The northgoing stream outside the harbour starts at HW Dover $-1\frac{1}{2}$, and reaches a peak of 2.1 knots (mean springs) at $+1$. The southgoing stream starts at HW Dover $+4\frac{1}{2}$, and reaches a peak of 2.1 knots (mean springs) at $-4\frac{1}{2}$.

The River Canche, Le Touquet and Etaples

Chart No. 2451

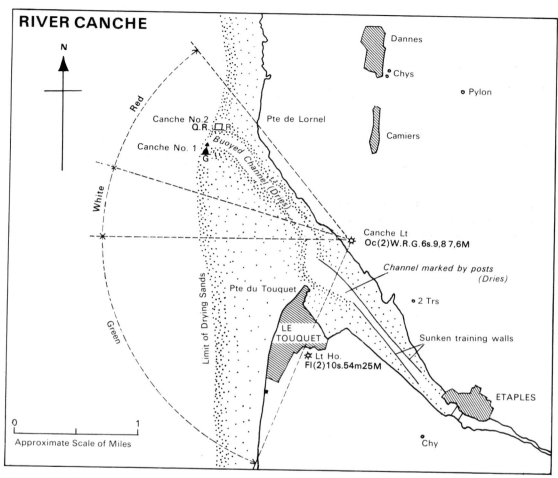

RIVER CANCHE

N

Red

Dannes

Chys

Pylon

Canche No.2
Q.R. R.

Pte de Lornel

Canche No. 1

Buoyed Channel (Dries)

G

Camiers

White

Canche Lt
Oc(2)W.R.G.6s.9,8 7,6M

Channel marked by posts
(Dries)

Green

Pte du Touquet

Limit of Drying Sands

2 Trs

LE
TOUQUET

Sunken training walls

Lt Ho.
Fl(2)10s.54m25M

ETAPLES

0   1

Approximate Scale of Miles

Chy

Plan 4   The River Canche, Le Touquet and Etaples.

This is a difficult and potentially dangerous river, which should only be visited in reasonable weather by yachtsmen experienced in shallow water navigation, and in a reasonably shallow draft vessel. On no account should the entrance be attempted in strong onshore winds, when the whole estuary becomes a mass of boiling surf, particularly once the ebb has begun. It is an interesting place, however, and well worth a visit in fine weather by those who enjoy exploring off the beaten track. A reliable echo-sounder is essential equipment.

There is at least 1½ m in the channel as far as Le Touquet, and 1 m on to Etaples, at HW on an extreme neap, with at least 2 more at HW on a good spring.

Entrance

The channel begins at the north end of the estuary, not far south of Pte. de Lornel, and the intending visitor should arrive at the entrance buoys not earlier than two hours or later than one hour before HW Etaples. Ideally, a visit should be planned near springs, but when the tides are still making. Halfway to springs, there is over 2 m in the Etaples channel, and if one has the misfortune to go aground at HW, one has at least avoided the danger of being neaped.

In good visibility, and one should not be attempting the entrance otherwise, there should be no difficulty in identifying the first pair of channel buoys, which at the recommended state of the tide will be in about 8 m of water. As shown on the Plan, No. 1 is green conical with a north cone topmark, and No. 2 a red pillar. From there the channel is well buoyed, although care must be taken to keep going for the nearest pair of buoys, and not cut any corners.

Le Touquet—Berthing and Facilities

Only boats that can dry in the open can stay in Le Touquet. There may be a free mooring, otherwise anchor just west of the moorings, taking local advice if possible, as there are one or two stone patches. Do not try to walk ashore without advice, as there are patches of quicksand and deep mud.

The YC (Cercle Nautique du Touquet) is very friendly and hospitable, it is open at weekends all the year round and every day in July and August: snack meals are available (except Saturday evenings) and there are toilets and showers; Tel. (21) 05-12-77.

There is usually someone there who can advise on a proposed visit. The town (¾ mile) has moderate shops but good restaurants: for good value keep well away from the sea front.

Etaples—Berthing and Facilities

Opposite the clubhouse at Le Touquet, the channel buoys give way to R and G posts, to be left respectively to port and starboard. These mark the best water in the channel, which runs

Plan 5 A view from the NW of the YC du Touquet on the Pointe du Touquet. The channel buoys are seen on the left, and Etaples is visible in the centre background. The pier in the foreground is now partially destroyed. *Reproduced by kind permission of the artist, Petit-Paul of St Valéry-sur-Somme.*

20

between two sunken training walls to Etaples. They are set wide apart, but near neaps if the best water must be found, it is necessary to zigzag between them, visiting each in turn. However, with moderate draft on a decent tide this is not necessary, but keep the echo sounder running continuously, and watch out for cross sets.

8. Le Touquet from the anchorage: the yacht club is near the right. There is plenty of room to anchor and good holding, but look out for the few stones.

There is a considerable fishing fleet operating from Etaples, and berthing depends very much on its movements. If the fleet is out, and remains so, there is a good long quay against which one can moor comfortably, and take the ground in a bilge-keeler, or in a keel boat with appropriate precautions. However, if the fleet arrives, one must cast off, and moor alongside one of them after they have settled. But either way it is a comfortable berth, sheltered in all conditions, and with the sort of facilities one would expect of a small fishing port. No specific yacht facilities, but visitors, particularly foreign ones, are unusual, and we are made to feel very welcome.

Etaples offers excellent shopping close to the harbour, with a particularly good fish market and a good vegetable one nearby.

Note: No entry is provided for the Baie de l'Authie, as this is a dangerous and extremely shallow estuary where little yachting takes place. There are forty or so local shallow-draft boats, and a few buoys and other marks are maintained, but the entrance is extremely tricky and only navigable by very shallow draft boats with up to date local knowledge.

Pilotage: Baie de Somme (Le Hourdel, Le Crotoy and St. Valéry-sur-Somme)

Chart No. 2612

General

The prerequisite for navigation of all craft of whatever size and for whatever purpose is water—sufficient water to float! Unfortunately the Baie de Somme does not offer this. In fact the whole of the area for about five miles in a N-S direction at its mouth and extending around eight miles inland E-W, dries out completely. Deep fissures and gullies are left in the soft mud when the tide recedes. The unfortunate result is that what might otherwise be a yachtsman's paradise should be strictly avoided by keel boats whose skippers are not experienced.

For the experienced yachtsman, however, who is used to shallow water sailing, and is not dismayed by the sight of a seagull's kneecaps as it stands in a few inches of water only a yard or two outside the channel, the area is well worth a visit, and indeed its principal port of St. Valéry-sur-Somme is one of the prettiest and most interesting towns on the whole coast. The entrance has a bad reputation, but in fact, although it is extremely rough and wet in onshore winds over force 4, it is quite safe for a seaworthy and well-found yacht in winds up to force 6, as long as entrance is made between two and one hours before high water. In such conditions, the sea remains rough until buoy 16.

There are three harbours, Le Hourdel, Le Crotoy and St. Valéry-sur-Somme and all three have small fishing fleets. In addition St. Valéry has, at any one time, accommodation for two or three cargo ships of around 800 tons. St. Valéry is reputed to have had 400 ships of William the Conqueror's fleet here for his invasion of England in 1066, but many of the ports along the coast make similar claims, and, in any case, this book is not a historical work, so other fascinating matters (for instance, Joan of Arc at Le Crotoy and traces of a Roman camp at St. Valéry) must be put aside. In general terms it is prudent to tackle the Baie de Somme not only in reasonable weather (as already mentioned) but also in daylight (few buoys are lighted), not before three-quarter flood and preferably not near the top of springs, for fear of being neaped. The echo sounder should be in constant use or the leadsman working non-stop.

Approach and Entrance

It cannot be too strongly emphasised that radical shifts in the position of the sandbanks in the estuary of the Somme take place from time to time, and both the plan and these notes must be used with this possibility constantly in mind. However, in calm weather or in offshore winds the entrance should present no problems. Coming from either direction, keep about a mile offshore until the beginning of the bay; then steer 15° or 210° (mag.) as appropriate until buoy ATSO is identified. If from there the first pair of channel buoys can be seen, make for them. If not, in reasonable weather it is perfectly safe to steer E until the water shoals to less than 6 m (for those with echo sounders in feet, say 20 ft) by which time the buoys should be clearly visible. The first pair of buoys are likely to be the ones furthest to the S, unless there is a really major change in

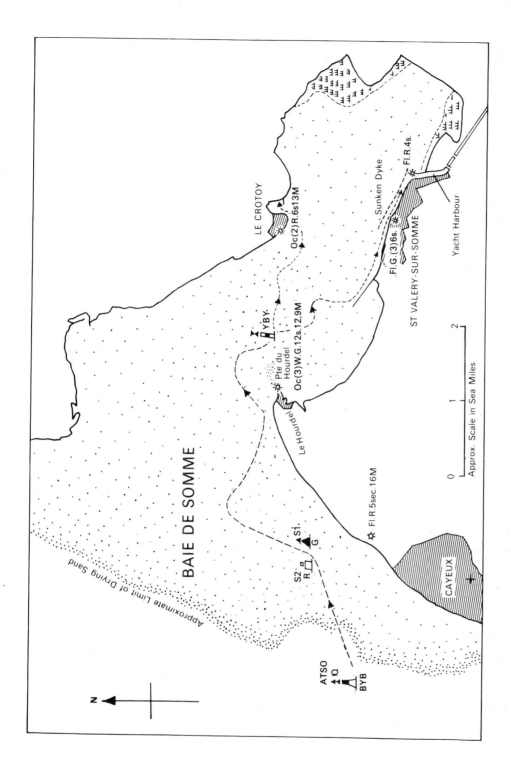

Plan 6 Sketch plan of Baie de Somme, showing position of offing and entrance buoys in 1982. *Warning:* substantial position changes may occur owing to shifting of the sands. (The dotted line — → — shows the general lie of the entrance channels — positions approximate and liable to change.) Principal lights only are shown.

23

the channel. Once in the channel, it is very closely buoyed, and there are no problems, but helmsmen should constantly keep an eye on the last pair of buoys passed as well as the next ones, to guard against being set out of the channel by cross currents. Buoys 1, 9, 15, 23 and 30 are lit, but no one in their senses would attempt an entry in the dark without first exploring in daylight.

In calm weather a shallow draft vessel can safely begin the passage from ATSO three hours before HW, but if there is any sea to speak of it is wiser to delay until two hours before. In onshore winds over force 4, it is unwise to leave ATSO later than one hour before, as the seas become dangerous once the tide turns. As a guide to timings, in 1977 it took me exactly 30 minutes from ATSO to A1, the first channel buoy, sailing at about 5 knots. From there to A16, where we got into shelter from the fairly heavy seas, took a further 24 minutes, and thence to the channel division buoy another 18 minutes. In all, from ATSO to St Valéry took 124 minutes, making an average of $4\frac{1}{2}$ knots through the water, so it will be seen that two hours before HW at ATSO is the ideal timing. There is usually at least 8 ft in the channel to St Valéry at HW neaps.

Harbours and Berthing

There are three ports where yachts may berth within the estuary: Le Hourdel, near the mouth, and Le Crotoy and St Valéry-sur-Somme, which face each other across the estuary about two miles inland. The usefulness of the three is in reverse order, with St Valéry being the most useful and providing the best facilities, and Le Hourdel the least. All three harbours are approached from the YBY channel division buoy which lies due E of Pte. du Hourdel.

9. Le Hourdel: the lighthouse and fishing boat quay at $1\frac{1}{2}$ hours before LW.

Le Hourdel

This small drying fishing port lies along the southern side of Pte. du Hourdel. The few moorings are too light for any but the smallest yachts, and visitors should berth alongside as space allows. The channel is unmarked and tricky. Leave the channel and steer for Pte de Hourdel when it is bearing SE, then round the point (sounding to avoid the spit which extends from it to the ENE) and enter the harbour, keeping close inshore once round the spit. Constant sounding is advisable. No facilities.

Le Crotoy

This port, whose name is pronounced as if spelt Crotois (i.e. Crotwa), is entered by the more northerly of the two buoyed channels that lead on from the division buoy. Buoy numbers are prefixed C, and in 1982 ran up to C10. The red ones are low with prominent topmarks, and so easily distinguishable from the large cans in the St Valéry channel. From the last buoy steer for the fishing boat quay, pass close along it and on round the wall until north of the spherical green buoy. Only then is it safe to steer for the pontoons. Moor in any vacant berth as available, and confirm at the club. There are 288 berths, 70 dredged to 1–2 m: the first day was free (1982), but subsequent ones rather expensive: a two day stay worked out about average for the area.

The yacht club is always open around high water, and for most of the day in July and August: showers (primitive but hot!) and toilets in the yard behind the club.

The approach channel is shallower than that to St Valéry: I found 6 ft at HW in 1979 on a medium tide (5·4 m at Dunkerque). As with all these shallow estuaries, it is safest to visit two or

10. Le Hourdel harbour from the moorings at HW. Moor alongside.

SPHERICAL GREEN BUOY

11. le Crotoy: yacht harbour at LW. The mud spit is clearly visible. The jetty is now solid concrete.

three days before the top of springs to avoid being neaped: this also results in a convenient mid-day high water.

St Valéry-sur-Somme

This is very much the best and most useful port in the estuary, as well as being an outstandingly beautiful town.

From the division buoy, the buoys (which run up to No. 50) and then a few lateral beacons must be followed closely to the harbour entrance. There are submerged walls at high water at both sides of the channel approaching the town, so it is important to keep closely to the fairway. As shown on the plan, there is a flashing green light on the starboard hand in the approach, and a red one at the end of the eastern wall of the harbour itself. Keep well over to the S side of the channel once the first houses of the town are abeam, crossing back to mid-channel as the R light tower comes abeam on the port side.

Continue up the harbour, past the berths for small coasters and fishing boats, and the yacht harbour comes into sight. This is of marina type, with mooring bow to pontoon and stern to buoy, but visitors usually moor to the ends of the pontoons, which have 6 ft at low water. When securing, allow for very strong stream on the ebb. Do not fail to get a key from the 'guardien' (on duty only HW $\pm$ 2) as the pontoons are permanently locked. Deposit 40 fr. (1982), returnable on

26

12. Le Crotoy: from the W at high tide. The sluice gates are on the right.

13. St Valéry-sur-Somme: the harbour entrance.

payment of the moderate dues. The marina is owned and operated by the Yacht Club S.N.V. (Sport Nautique Valericain).

There are no facilities or toilets in the marina. Hall Nautique de la Baie de Somme, have a first class chandlery, and can do repairs to motors, hulls or electrics, but not sails. For help or advice, contact Paul Petit, who has a hardware shop and gallery (of his own pictures) on the quay. Telephone (22)27-51-27. Restaurants are rather touristy and very expensive, so it is worth recording that there is an excellent small family concern in the shape of the Brasserie de la Ferté, 15 Rue de la Ferté.

It is possible to lock into the canal to Abbeville, but it is little used by yachts, and the bridges may not open unless there is a cargo vessel passing through. The lock gates are above the marina. Enquire of the lock-keeper, who lives in the first house on the left bank above the first bridge. Throughout the channel, priority must be given to commercial and fishing vessels.

No tidal data are given for this area, as all depths and soundings are uncertain and liable to change. East winds can lower the level of tides by up to 0·3 metres, and currents can be strong: on an average spring tide the ebb attains 5 knots off Le Hourdel.

14. St Valéry-sur-Somme: continuation of the same channel at low water, and yacht moorings. At the far end of the picture is the lock into the Abbeville Canal.

28

15. St Valéry-sur-Somme: the same, but looking from near the bridge. To the left is the road and the offices of the *Ponts et Chaussées*.

Le Tréport

Charts Nos. 2612 and 1351

This is a perfectly charming little town, and well worth a visit, although the facilities for yachtsmen are unfortunately very poor, and strangers would be well advised to avoid making their first visit at night.

Le Tréport lies on the NE border of Normandy (indeed the yacht club and lock control tower lie in Picardy) and the name is thought to derive from the Latin 'Ulterior Portus'. During its long history it has been burnt down by the English four times (1339, 1413, 1513, and 1545), and occupied by the Germans twice (1870 and 1940), but there are still many beautiful buildings of different periods, which blend together to give the town great character. The surroundings of the Bassin á Flot, however, where yachts must lie, are noisy, dirty and ugly, and there are no facilities at all for the visiting yachtsman, who may even find considerable difficulty in getting ashore as the level in the basin drops alarmingly while the tide is out, and there are few ladders in the areas where yachts are allowed to moor.

Ideally, entrance to the harbour should be made between two hours before until two hours after HW Dieppe, but there may be one or more additional hours each side, depending on draft and sea conditions generally. There is severe scend in the Avant Port in onshore winds, so it is not safe to dry out in such conditions if late for the lock. Dieppe, 14 miles to the SW is the only safe—if uncomfortable—alternative.

150 M

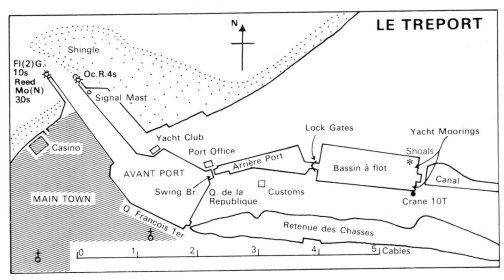

Plan 7   Sketch plan of Le Tréport harbour. Not to exact scale.

16. Le Tréport: the entrance, showing the lighthouse on the western breakwater.

Identification

In common with many ports on this coast, Le Tréport can be difficult to identify as like so many others it has high cliffs on each side. The cliffs to the SW end rather abruptly, and the ones to the NE taper down more gradually; at the foot of each is a clock tower. In reasonable visibility it is usually possible to pick out the lighthouse on the west pierhead. This is white with a black base and top, and is fairly conspicuous. The sight of this tower removes any doubts, as no other coastal town in this area has anything similar. At night, the lighthouse has a good light, Fl, (2) G 10s, visible 12 miles. The illuminated crucifix on the cliffs south of the entrance is also visible for many miles at night. In bad visibility the fog signal (Reed Mo. (N) 30s) can be a help in finding the entrance.

Approach and Entrance

Entrance should only be attempted at above half tide: local advice is not to enter within $3\frac{1}{2}$ hours of low water, either before or after. Tides are 6 minutes after Dieppe, so the Dieppe tables can be used for most purposes.

As one is unlikely to wish to enter after the lock gates have closed, in practice the ideal time for entry is from $2\frac{1}{2}$ hours to a few minutes before H.W. Dieppe. Approach is straightforward, as long as the existence of the tongue of shingle extending NW from the E pierhead is remembered. Make for a position $\frac{1}{2}$ mile NW of the pierheads, and from there steer south until

31

the light on the east pier is almost in line with the light on the west pierhead. From here it is safe to steer for the west pierhead, keeping the east light just open of the (much larger) west light. Once round the west pierhead proceed down the centre of the channel into the Avant-Port.

17. Le Tréport: the outer harbour near LW. The harbour master's office is shown at 'X'.

Berthing

If one has arrived in the Avant-Port too early for the lock gates to be open, it may be possible to pick up a mooring, or alternatively one may tie up alongside the NE wall, near the Port Office (see plan). The lock gates open between two and one hours before high water, according to the level of the tide, and close exactly at high water. During that time the swing bridge opens on request: in theory the signal is three blasts on the horn, but in practice this is seldom necessary, as a good lookout is kept, at least during daylight hours. Once the bridge opens, pass straight through the Arriere-Port, and berth in the Bassin à Flot. The long sides of this basin are reserved for the considerable cargo vessels which use the port, and yachts are usually directed to berth at the east end of the basin, often alongside a fishing boat. Beware shoal water in the NE corner of the basin (see plan), and sound carefully before deciding on a mooring, bearing in mind that the water level can drop by as much as six feet between the closure of the lock and its next opening. The photograph shows what *can* happen. It is sometimes possible to berth at the west end, which is more comfortable and nearer the town. Apart from a crane (see plan) there are no yacht facilities. Good shopping and restaurants in the town. The Yacht Club de la Bresle is only active at weekends in the season. For general information, apply to the Syndicat d'Initiative at the Casino. Customs office on Quai Edouard-Gelée, tel. (35) 86-15-34. Some chandlery and repairs available from Chantiers Naval du Tréport, Quai Sud, just E of the basin.

32

In 1982 works were in progress for the building of a new lock and bridge. This may eventually lead to the creation of a new yacht harbour, but the immediate effect is to make life more difficult, with Heath Robinson swing bridges and a great deal of mess and noise. Until things are cleared up it would be most unwise for a stranger to enter at night, as the general level of lighting is very poor, and there are many dangerous obstructions along the sides of the channel into the Arrière Port.

18. Remember to allow for the fall in water level between tides at Le Tréport.

Tidal information

HEIGHT ABOVE DATUM OF SOUNDINGS IN METRES

High water		*Low water*	
Mean springs	Mean neaps	Mean springs	Mean neaps
10·1	7·9	1·3	3·0

For tidal streams see Dieppe, from which there is no significant difference.

Dieppe

Chart Nos. 2612 and 2147

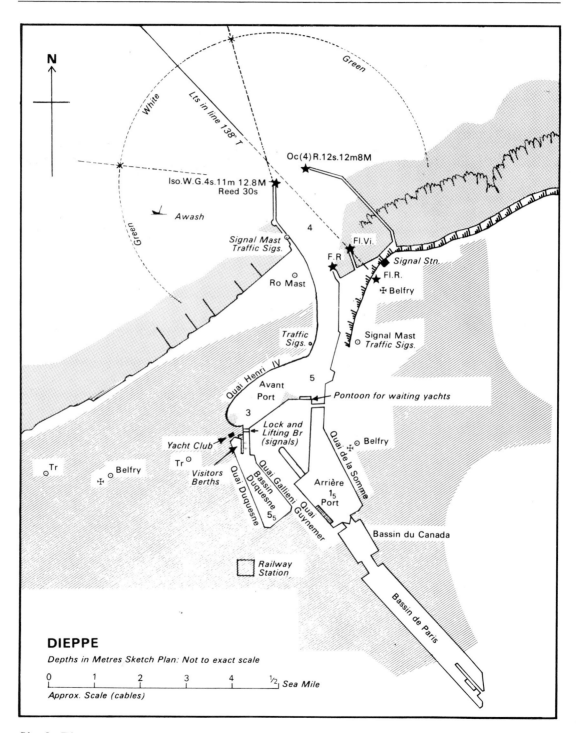

N

Green

White

Lts in line 138° T

Green

Oc(4)R.12s.12m8M

Iso.W.G.4s.11m 12.8M
Reed 30s

Awash

4

Signal Mast
Traffic Sigs.

Fl.Vi.

F.R

Signal Stn.

Ro Mast

Fl.R.

Belfry

Traffic
Sigs.

Signal Mast
Traffic Sigs.

Quai Henri IV

Avant
Port

5

Pontoon for waiting yachts

3

Lock and
Lifting Br
(signals)

Yacht Club

Belfry

Tr

Tr

Belfry

Visitors
Berths

Quai Duquesne

Quai Gallieni

Bassin
Duquesne
5₅

Quai Guynemer

Arrière
1₅
Port

Quai de la Somme

Bassin du Canada

Railway
Station

Bassin de Paris

DIEPPE

Depths in Metres Sketch Plan: Not to exact scale

| 0 | 1 | 2 | 3 | 4 | ¹/₂ Sea Mile |

Approx. Scale (cables)

Plan 8   Dieppe.

19. Dieppe: entrance to the outer harbour.

The tidal part of Dieppe harbour is in the highest degree commercial; ferries, freighters, hydrofoils and fishing boats dodge each other, in no way inclined to treat yachts as anything but a nuisance. There is a yacht pontoon, but this is very much a token gesture: it is at best uncomfortable, and at worst dangerous, as the swell in northerly winds reaches it almost unbroken. However, there is an excellent, welcoming and comfortable yacht harbour in the Bassin Duquesne, so all one has to do is try to arrive at a time that enables one to lock in with a minimum of delay.

Identification and Entrance to the Harbour

Dieppe sprawls, as opposed to small harbours, which nestle, where the cliffs on each side stop rather abruptly. There is often a haze over the town and harbour. It is a busy port and there are ferries to and from Newhaven, also there is always the activity of the fishing fleet; if vessels of this size are sighted it is a good indication that Dieppe is ahead.

In good visibility a chateau with a tower may be seen on the western side of the town, built half-way up the cliff. Next, to eastwards, is the church of St Jacques which is sited prominently about the centre of the town and very close to the outer harbour. To the north of the harbour and on the cliffs is another prominent church, Notre Dame de Bon-Secours.

Entrance to the harbour is simple and in normal conditions a yacht can safely approach from any direction and steer straight in between the pierheads. In strong onshore winds near LW, however, the entrance should be approached on a course of roughly 140° True (say 145° mag.).

35

There is an important warning about the entrance which must be made here; the traffic signals must be strictly followed. Towards low water there is literally no room for a yacht when a ferry is coming out. The correct procedure is to wait outside the harbour until the traffic signals change. If through any mischance a yachtsman should find it imperative to make harbour against the signals then there is just space inside the entrance on the starboard side.

However, to enter at all against the signals is against the regulations, and unless a proper reason can be given ('It was rough out there' is not enough!), action may be taken. The signals are as follows:

	Red	Green	Green
Lights	White	White	White
	Red	Green	Red
Meaning	No entry	No departure	No entry or departure

20. Dieppe: yacht moorings in Bassin Duquesne. The Yacht Club is to the left and the lock gates and lifting bridge to the right of centre

36

In anything except bad visibility the entrance is easy and no difficulties should be experienced. Harbour control operates on VHF Channel 12.

Once inside, keep fairly close in along the starboard (western) wall, following it round to starboard into the main Avant Port. Here is the visitors' pontoon which may be used for a period of one tide, but use your strongest warps and biggest fenders.

It is also possible to lie against the wall SW of the pontoon, but this is rough and warps must be tended constantly owing to the considerable rise and fall of tide. Fishing boats tend to be unwelcoming, and if mooring to one the boat must be left crewed and ready to move immediately.

The lock into the Bassin Duquesne opens 2 hours before HW, and closes between 1.05 hours after (low neaps) and 1.25 hours after (high springs). The bridge will open two or three times during the open period: signal two blasts if necessary. One G light permits entry to the basin, one R departure, RG together no passage. Turn sharp to starboard at the end of the entrance channel to enter the part of the basin reserved for yachts. The yacht club is just W of the lifting bridge: the steward will advise on mooring and collect dues. It has a tiny bar, and a small but well-kept toilet and shower. There is a 3-ton crane in the basin, and water and electricity are available.

Diesel is normally available in cans only from Marchand & Co, about 100 m NW from the clubhouse on Quai Duquesne. They will lend cans. For 500 litres or more the club can arrange delivery by lorry alongside in the Bassin Duquesne or, near high water, in the Avant Port.

Chandlery can be found at Guillard-Marine, 24 Rue de la Mariniere (Tel. (35) 84-14-42), but major repairs are probably best handled by M. Alexandre Lefebvre of Dieppe Nautic, on the Route Etran, a little way out at Neuville-les-Dieppe (Tel. 84-13-80). Excellent and relatively cheap restaurants are to be found near the yacht harbour, on the whole the Quai Duquesne having the more expensive ones and the Quai Henri Quatre the cheaper.

Duty-free stores are obtainable from Etablissement Olivier, 15 rue Jehan-Veron. Customs office in rue Descroisilles, (Tel. 84-24-57).

Tidal information on next page.

HEIGHT ABOVE DATUM OF SOUNDINGS IN METRES

High water		Low water	
Mean springs	Mean neaps	Mean springs	Mean neaps
9·1	7·1	0·6	2·4

The NE stream begins at HW Dover $-4\frac{1}{2}$, and attains a maximum of 1.7 knots (mean springs) at -3. The SW stream starts at HW Dover $+1\frac{1}{4}$, and reaches a maximum of 1.2 knots (mean springs) at $+4$.

St Valéry-en-Caux

Chart No. 2612

St Valéry-en-Caux is one of the most active yachting centres in East Normandy, and has excellent facilities for visiting yachtsmen.

The town has an ancient history, going back to the 7th Century, when the inhabitants were converted to Christianity by Saint Valéry himself and his monks from St Valéry-sur-Somme.

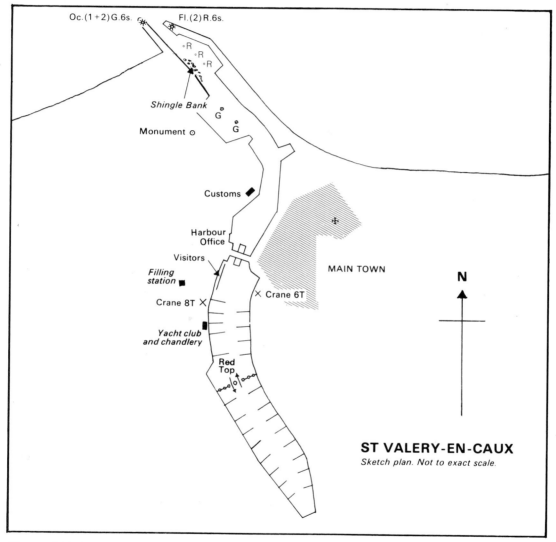

Plan 9 St Valéry-en-Caux.

The relics of the saint were brought here by Richard the Lionheart in 1197, although they were removed not long after. In 1940, General Rommel destroyed the eastern part of the town with artillery when the 51st Highland Division refused to surrender. The name means St Valéry in the chalk, the old county of Caux having taken its name from the ancient word for the area's most visible mineral.

Identification

Arriving from the open sea, really good dead reckoning and attention to tidal streams are necessary because nearly all the harbours on this coast appear the same from 5 miles away; St Valéry is no exception, being in a valley where there is a break in the cliffs. The best landmark is the nuclear power station at Port Susette, about three miles west of the town. It is also sometimes possible to pick out the red and white radio mast which stands just to the east of the town. Coming from the east, there is also a conspicuous white vertical stripe on the cliff which lies just beyond the harbour. Particularly when approaching from the west, the town itself is invisible until it is very nearly abeam, as it lies well back in a fairly narrow gap in the cliffs. The lighthouse on the end of the west pier is white with a green top.

21. St Valéry-en-Caux. Keep further to port than the yacht shown entering until past the wave-break gap on the port side.

40

Approach and Entrance

The western mole extends further out to sea than the eastern one, to give craft that are making harbour some protection against the prevailing westerlies. This however produces bad turbulence on the more rare occasions when there is a north easterly wind. Wind from between north and east over force 5 causes severe sea conditions, and entry should not be attempted at such times. To act as a wave-breaker, there is a slope on the east mole which takes the sting out of the sea by absorbing and smoothing the waves. Unfortunately it has the effect of collecting a big bank of shingle on the western side of the entrance which it is most important to avoid. The approach to the harbour is 150° (mag.) which is when the lighthouse on the western mole and the light structure on the eastern mole are in line. When abeam of the lighthouse on the western mole it is of great importance to close the eastern mole and take a course parallel to it. Between the eastern light structure and the mole proper there are three posts with red tops which mark the ramp. They should be left close to port as the shingle bank lies opposite them.

After successfully negotiating the entrance and the short channel leading to the outer harbour, visitors arriving outside opening hours will generally find a mooring available to pick up while waiting for the lock gates to open. The outer harbour should only be entered three hours either side of high water, and the lock gates open $2\frac{3}{4}$ hours either side, except at extreme neaps, when this is reduced to 2 hours either side. The wait is therefore unlikely to be a long one. During the time the gates are open the bridge opens every half hour (except between 1200 and

22. St Valéry-en-Caux: the yacht basin looking towards the lifting bridge and lock.

41

1300), so the sounding of horns is useless and unpopular. A limited service is operated at night (15.6–15.9 only) with only two bridge openings, $\frac{1}{2}$ hour before and $\frac{1}{4}$ hour after HW. A green light at the bridge allows entry, a red light departure; RG means no passage.

The entrance channel carries 2 metres of water at half tide, so entrance times must be adjusted to the circumstances, and in strong onshore winds it is wiser to postpone entry until $1\frac{1}{2}$ hours before high water, by which time the depth in the channel is 4 metres or more.

Berthing

On entering the inner harbour, a pontoon will be seen immediately to starboard after passing through the lock. This is the Ponton d'Acceuil, and visitors should tie up here temporarily and enquire for a berth. Note that as shown on the plan, the wet basin is divided in half by a sunken beam which joins a series of concrete supports originally intended for a bridge. The passage is clear either side of the central post, identified by a red top.

Facilities and General

The old Yacht Club building had been demolished by 1982, and a new one was under construction, scheduled for completion June/July 1983. There will be toilets and showers on the ground floor and club rooms on the second. The first floor will be occupied by the port's excellent yacht chandler, Alain Bondois (Tel. (35) 97-04-22). They undertake repairs, and are competent, fast, and reasonably priced. There are two cranes which can handle weights of up to 8 tons. There is no grid, but a small concrete slip exists in the outer harbour, near the lock gates. The president of the yacht club, M. Leseigneur, who lives on the Quai d'Amont on the east side of the outer harbour, is most friendly and helpful. Customs on the Quai d'Aval: Tel. 97-04-64. Diesel from the filling station shown on the plan (closed Wednesdays). Alain Bondois will lend cans. With 600 berths, this is one of the most important yachting centres in the area. Excellent shopping and restaurants in the town.

Tidal Information

Range at Mean springs: 7·7 metres; at .Mean neaps: 4·7 metres. The west-going stream begins at HW Dover $+\frac{1}{2}$, and reaches a maximum rate of 1·5 knots at HW Dover $+4$. The east-going stream starts at HW Dover $-5\frac{1}{2}$, and attains a maximum of 2·4 knots (mean springs) at HW Dover $-2\frac{1}{2}$.

Fécamp

Charts Nos. 2612 and 1351

Fécamp has a thirteenth-century church, Notre Dame du Salut, and is renowned for the Benedictine liqueur made in the town. The museum at the distillery is well worth a visit.

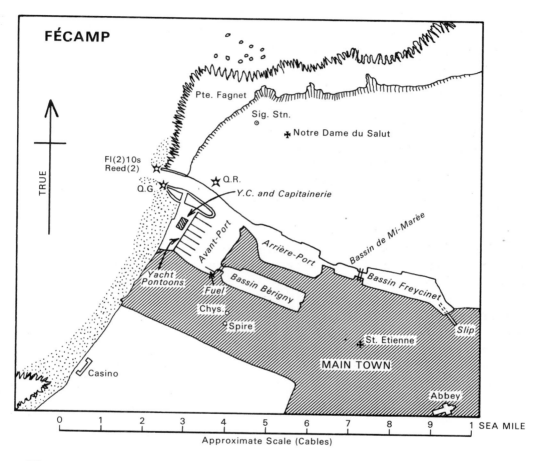

Plan 10 Fécamp.

Identification

To the east of the harbour, on top of the cliffs of Pte. Fagnet, is the church of Notre Dame du Salut, and also a signal station, which looks from a distance rather like a lighthouse. In the town

43

itself there are two towers, the one with a sloping top being on the Abbey, and a water tower. Further to starboard is the chimney of the Benedictine factory, and the delicately pointed spire of its bell-tower nearby.

Approach and Entry

The entrance to Fécamp can be rough in winds of force 5 or more from the SW to NW, as the bottom shelves steeply, but with sufficient water entry is safe in anything short of a full gale. The approach and channel between the piers is kept dredged to 1·5 metres, but in rough weather it is wise to time one's entry for two hours either side of HW: one hour if the sea is very bad. If waiting outside it is wiser to heave-to or jill around, as the holding is poor.

The best line for entry is to approach the pierheads on a course of about 85° (mag.). When close in, keep more towards the S pierhead, particularly if entering well before HW, when there is a strong northerly set across the entrance.

23. Fécamp: the entrance and Pte. Fagnet.

Traffic signals are shown from a mast on the S jetty, and must be observed. A red flag or light means No Entry, a green flag or light No Departure, and both shown together prohibits all movement.

Once between the piers, keep to the centre of the channel as far as traffic will allow, and if under sail beware of strong gusts from unexpected directions. Take the first large opening on the starboard hand into the Avant Port, which is now the yacht harbour.

44

Berthing

The Avant Port at Fécamp is now completely given over to yachts, and provides first class pontoon moorings with all facilities. The visitors pontoon is the fourth one on the starboard hand (marked 'C'), which provides twenty or more places in the outer half which is reserved for visitors. Failing a vacancy here, tie up where there is a gap and report to the Capitainerie in the large building above the pontoons, where a berth will be allotted. This is seldom necessary, however, as the harbourmaster is very active, and usually signals visitors to a suitable berth. Care should be taken when mooring, as considerable scend can develop in the harbour in winds from the western quadrant. For this reason, and also because it is cheaper, visitors planning a long stay, or leaving their boat, are advised to arrange to lock into the Bassin Bérigny, where one can lie alongside in perfect shelter.

Facilities and General

Facilities in Fécamp are excellent. There is a ramp and grid in the N corner of the Avant-Port, and a slip in the Bassin Freycinet. Among the numerous establishments, Moré et Cie. stand out, as they provide virtually all services except sailmaking and repair. They have a small wooden shop NE of the Capitainerie, but their main workshops are on the Quai de Verdun, on the south side of the Bassin Freycinet. For advice on specialised services, ask at the Capitainerie.

Petrol and Diesel are available from a pontoon on the SE side of the Avant Port, just NE of the lock into the Bassin Bérigny, 0900–1130 and 1500–1800; closed Thursdays. Water and electricity on the pontoons. A 35 ton mobile crane is also available.

24. Fécamp: the entrance and Avant Port from Notre Dame du Salut.

25. Fécamp: yacht pontoons in the Avant-Port. The yacht club and Capitainerie share the conspicuous building on the skyline.

There are a few restaurants down by the harbour, and as long as M. Benvides remains owner of the Hotel du Progres on Quai Vicomte, it can be especially recommended; but the best food and shops are to be found up in the main part of the town, between the church of St Etienne and the Abbey itself (not to be confused with the factory which in spite of its elegant spire is in a rather slummy area). This is about a mile from the yacht harbour, but well worth the walk.

The yacht club, the Société des Regates de Fécamp, shares a building with the Capitainerie, and is large and comfortable and friendly. Good showers, toilets and washrooms are provided, and the bar has a splendid view of the coast.

Useful telephone numbers for the port include: Yacht Club, (35) 28-08-44; Capitainerie, 28-13-58; Customs, 28-19-40; Weather Forecast (automatic answering service, 3 bulletins per day), 42-12-19 or 42-14-35.

Tidal information
Range at Mean springs: 7·3 metres; at Mean neaps: 4·3 metres.

For tidal streams see St Valéry-en-Caux, from which the streams differ little.

46

Pilotage—Le Havre to Fécamp

The main feature on this passage is the enormous new oil-tanker terminal which lies just south of Cap D'Antifer. The main breakwater lies to the north of the harbour, and extends some $1\frac{1}{2}$ miles from the shore, first NW and then W, before turning SSW for a further $\frac{1}{2}$ mile. There is a QR. (20m, 10 M.) on the end of this main breakwater, and numerous other lit buoys mark the channel. There are also many other lights on the breakwater and ashore. The area can be very confusing at night, and even in the daytime it should be given a wide berth, perhaps a mile outside the end of the breakwater, as vessels enter and leave quickly and without warning, and cannot slow down or deviate from their course.

Apart from the area of Antifer, there are no offshore hazards, and in settled weather most of the passage can safely be made $\frac{1}{2}$ mile offshore, but with an onshore wind of any strength it is prudent to keep rather further off. Leaving Le Havre going north, or approaching it from the north, there is no need to go right out to the end of the deep-water channel, as the waters around Cap de la Hève are well buoyed, enabling the yachtsman safely to keep close in and join or leave the main channel only a mile or so west of the entrance to Le Havre Avant-Port.

The only hazard for which it is necessary to keep an eye out is the Banc de l'Eclat, which lies about $1\frac{1}{2}$ miles from the harbour entrance just north of the channel, and close WNW of buoy L.H. 14 (Oc R 4s). If when coming south one keeps close in under Cap de la Hève, say $\frac{1}{4}$ to $\frac{1}{2}$ mile off, and then steers 160° (mag.) one will come down on the last of the port buoys, L.H. 16 (Oc (2) R 6s), well inside all dangers. Similarly going north, one can turn north on a course to leave Cap de la Hève close to starboard as soon as one has reached L.H.16.

Going north and east, it is easy to identify Pte. Fagnet, just beyond the entrance to Fécamp, from Yport, the white signal station on top of the cliffs being conspicuous and clearly visible from this direction. A feature of this whole coast, but especially noticeable on this stretch, is that the towns (in this case Etretat and Yport) are totally invisible until almost abeam. It can worry the navigator who sees a large town marked on the chart but an apparently unbroken line of chalk cliffs stretching into the distance.

Le Havre

Charts Nos. 2990, 2146 and 2613

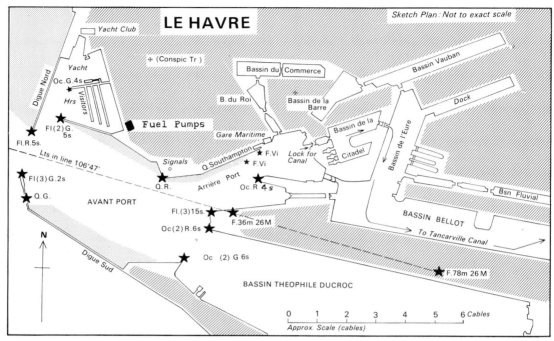

Plan 11 Le Havre

Le Havre, its name derived from 'Havre de Grace,' which was so badly battered in the last war, has been largely re-built to retain its place as the most important port on the north coast of France. It is a deep water port having its own yacht harbour and is a welcome sanctuary for yachtsmen: moreover it is accessible at all states of the tide.

The outer approach to Le Havre is marked by a Lanby buoy, about 10 miles W of the harbour entrance, RWVS, Fl (2) R 10s 10m 20 M, Siren (2) 60s; a useful aid if approaching from seaward. The buoy has a radio beacon, 296.5 kHz, in addition to a radar reflector. The transmitter is short range, about 10 miles, and transmits call sign BG (— ·· — —·) for 4 secs., followed by a tuning signal for 6 secs., then silence 10 secs., total 20 secs., and this is continuous.

Approaches and entrance to the harbour

The buoyed channel begins 6 miles from the entrance. The outer part of this is, however, seldom used by yachts except in poor visibility, and indeed, as with many channels leading into busy commercial ports, it is safer to keep just out of the fairway for as long as possible. There are

48

leading lights on 106° 47′ True, FW, visible 26 miles and bright enough to see by day, often cutting through poor visibility. This line leads through the pierheads, Fl (3) G 2s on the south mole and Fl R 5s (very bright) on the north mole.

The yacht harbour lies immediately to port after passing through the entrance, but it is important to keep at least 30 metres from the northern mole, as it has a collection of most unpleasant boulders piled along its eastern side. At night, steer to leave the light Fl (2) G 5s on the end of the nearer mole about 30 m to starboard, and then turn to starboard into the well-lit yacht harbour. Visitors should moor in the nearer of the two basins, stern to a buoy and bow to pontoon. The outer side of the first main pontoon is reserved for visitors.

The entrance at night has been carefully detailed and given first. The daylight entrance is easy and has been made even easier by the very big chimneys of the new power station, built in 1968, known locally as 'Central Thermique'. They are 247 m high, and can be seen a long way off. When entering and leaving the harbour, keep well over to your starboard side, but do not enter 'round the corner' without first looking in from well off the pierhead to see if the entrance is clear.

Berths and Facilities

As already stated, the visitors berths are on the outer side of the most westerly pontoon in the Anse de Joinville, which is the nearer (southernmost) of the two basins at the NW end of the Avant-Port. There is water on the pontoons, a 16 ton crane at the SE corner of the basin, and a slip in the NE corner of the inner basin, now called the Anse des Regates. The yacht club (Tel.

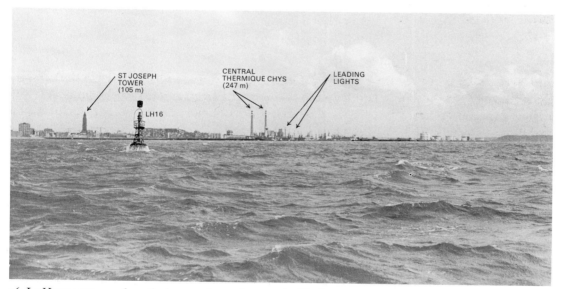

26. Le Havre: entrance from the last port buoy of approach. The Thermique Centrale chimneys are clearly visible.

(35) 42-41-21) and Capitainerie (Tel. 22-81-40) are on the northern side of the latter basin.

For a long stay, it is possible to make arrangements through the yacht club, the Société des Regates du Havre, to be let into the Bassin du Commerce, entered from the Arrière-Port. There are three bridges and a lock to be opened, however, so a day or two's notice is required.

All possible services can be found in Le Havre, including a sailmaker, Marc Phillippe (Voiles), on the Avenue Lucien-Corbeaux (Tel. 26-42-87). Almost all other services can be supplied by Manche Yachting, opposite the yacht harbour in the Rue des Sauveteurs (Tel. 21-08-06), but there are many other excellent chandlers and services of all kinds. Shopping is excellent, but the best areas are a fair step from the yacht basin. Charts from Heilmann, 23 Rue de Paris, Tel. 42-42-49. Fuel, both diesel and petrol, from the pumps in the SE corner of the yacht harbour: easiest near high water.

The yacht club is large, hospitable and rather grand. A reasonable standard of dress and behaviour is expected, which is hardly unreasonable for one of the leading clubs of France. It is open all the year round, and has a restaurant which offers excellent value. During the season there is also a secondary club-house at Ste.-Adresse, also with a restaurant, and offering a magnificent view of the whole estuary of the Seine. It is well worth a visit.

The Tancarville Canal

Basically this book does not include inland waterways, however, this canal may be of importance if

27. Le Havre: entrance to the Tancarville Canal.

a yacht wishes to reach the Seine without going into the estuary in conditions of gale force winds: a brief description is therefore given.

The approximate total distance from the Arrière Port to where the Canal joins the Seine is 25 kilometres. Apart from the locks at both ends there are twelve bridges and progress through the canal can only be described as tedious.

There is a choice of entrances to the Canal: the big lock for large craft is between the Quai d'Escole and the Quai des Remorquers. The small lock (for small craft) is at the extreme easterly end of the Arrière Port, just past the quay where the Thoresen ferries moor, which is on the Quai de Southampton.

After coming out of the lock proceed straight ahead and straight across the Bassin de la Citadelle and through a bridge (No. 2) into the Bassin L'Eure. Here turn smartly to starboard and proceed south as far as possible. At the final T junction, turn to port (E) and proceed to the end of the Bassin Bellot, through the bridge at its NE corner (No. 3) and one more just beyond into the Bassin Vetillart. After this keep straight on to bridge No. 5 and straight ahead to bridges Nos. 6, 7 and 8. There is still one more bridge, the Hode Bridge, some 12 km ahead, and then come eight kilometres of uninterrupted passage to the lock at the remote end of the Canal where it enters the Seine. The maximum speed laid down by the Authorities for the Tancarville Canal is 8 knots.

There is a small booklet or pocket almanac which may be of importance when using the Tancarville Canal, and indeed, Le Havre and the estuary of the Seine; it is entitled *La Mer* and is strongly recommended. Although only available in French, even with a limited knowledge of the language a yachtsman will be able, for instance, to use the special tide tables for the Seine giving the depths to be added to the chart datum *for every hour*. Moreover there are diagrams of the signalling systems employed for the different locks and it could be described as a miniature almanac which fits easily into the pocket, in spite of its 244 pages. It is not suggested that every yachtsman calling at Le Havre needs it, but anyone who intends spending some time in or around the Seine estuary could use much of the information in it to good advantage. It also contains a couple of pages of French/English nautical terms. *La Mer* is obtainable from Librairie Maritime Le Yacht, 55 Avenue de la Grande-Armée, Paris 16 me, or from Editeurs Micaux, 8–10 Impasse Greuze, Le Havre.

Tidal information

HEIGHT ABOVE DATUM OF SOUNDINGS IN METRES

High water		Low water	
Mean springs	Mean neaps	Mean springs	Mean neaps
7·8	6·4	1·0	2·7

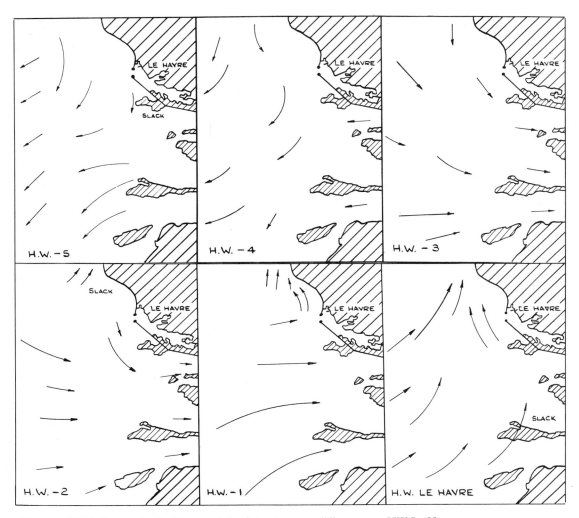

Plan 12 Tidal diagram for Le Havre and the Seine Estuary: differences on HW Le Havre.

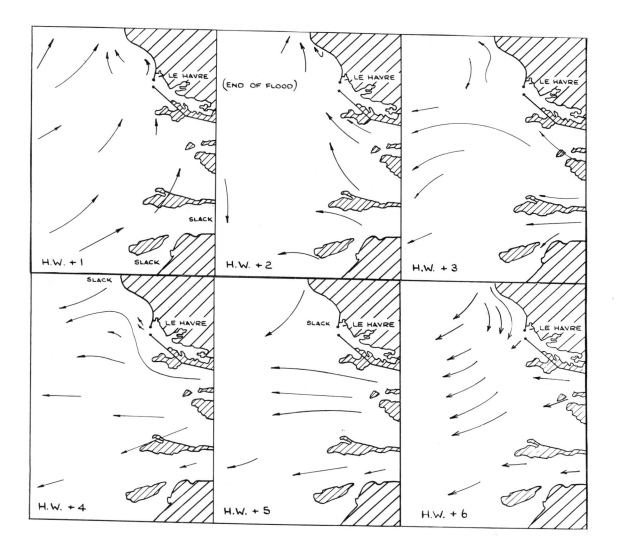

H.W. + 1

SLACK

SLACK

H.W. + 2

(END OF FLOOD)

SLACK

LE HAVRE

H.W. + 3

LE HAVRE

H.W. + 4

SLACK

LE HAVRE

H.W. + 5

SLACK

LE HAVRE

H.W. + 6

LE HAVRE

LE HAVRE

Pilotage: the Estuary of the Seine

Charts Nos. 2146 and 2990

The main feature of the estuary of the Seine used to be the occurrence of a very dangerous bore, known as the *mascaret*. However, extensive dredging and deepening of the channel, and the construction of submerged breakwaters, has reduced it to a shadow of its former self, and indeed it officially ceased to exist some years ago. However, the remnants can still in fact be observed at spring tides, and under suitable conditions it can be quite fierce between Quilleboeuf and La Mailleraye.

As with all passages on tidal rivers, achievement of a quick and successful run depends upon starting at exactly the right state of the tide. On passage to Rouen, one should aim to be off Honfleur about four hours before high water Le Havre, from where by maintaining something over five knots through the water, Rouen can be reached on a single flood tide.

As always, the downward trip is more difficult. The ebb can only be carried for about four hours before the new flood is met, when one is best advised to pick up the next practicable mooring and wait for the stream to slacken before continuing. The main force of the flood only lasts for 3–4 hours, so by this method it is usually easy to reach Honfleur or Le Havre in one day, riding down on two successive ebbs. The ideal time to leave Rouen is 10 hours after LW Le Havre: i.e. $4\frac{1}{2}$ hours after HW there.

Note that Honfleur is useless as a port of call on the way up to Rouen, as by the time he can leave the harbour, the yachtsman will have missed the best of the flood. To visit Honfleur in its own right (and nobody should miss it!), departure from either Le Havre or Deauville 2–3 hours before HW Le Havre will ensure arrival at a convenient time to lock straight in to the inner harbour. From Deauville, care must be taken to clear the west end of the Ratelets shoal, and thereafter keep north of the Digue du Ratier, marked at its west end by a beacon tower VQ, and subsequently by unlit posts. Similarly, coming from Le Havre, the west end of the Basse du Nord shoal must be cleared: this is achieved by keeping west of the *Amfard SW* buoy (Oc (2) R 6s).

Tidal diagrams for the mouth of the Seine will be found on pages 52 and 53.

Pilotage: the River Seine, Le Havre to Rouen

Yachtsmen who have taken their boats up to Rouen and back again to Le Havre have frequently been heard to exclaim that the whole exercise is dead easy. Indeed it can be simple, but it is necessary to take very careful account of the tides. In this chapter some of these tidal characteristics are examined, but in addition the only serious hazard of the Seine—bad visibility—and what action a yachtsman should take, are given consideration.

The tide

The distance between the Tancarville bridge (25 km. to Le Havre) and Rouen is 95 km., and roughly when it is low water at Le Havre it is high water at Rouen and vice-versa.

The golden rule when planning the voyage up the Seine is to start in plenty of time and, having started, not to stop, but to keep the engine running so as to maintain 6 knots if possible through the water, arriving at Rouen between 7–9 hours later during the very long high water which occurs both at Rouen and all places on the Seine between Le Havre and Rouen. In order to amplify this, the following table is given which is the information used by the river pilots. The figures are those which should be *added* to the times of *low water* Le Havre to find the times at which the flood and ebb streams begin at different places. These figures were originally derived from the Ponts et Chaussées diagrams of tidal behaviour of the Seine. Low water Le Havre can be taken to be 5·30 hours before HW, except for neaps (under 7·0 m) when 5·45 hours before is more accurate.

PLACE	FLOOD STREAM BEGINS (Hours after L.W. Le Havre)			EBB STREAM BEGINS (Hours after L.W. Le Havre)		
	SPRINGS	MID-TIDES	NEAPS	SPRINGS	MID-TIDES	NEAPS
La Roque	2·40	2·30	2·05	7·00	6·50	6·10
Quillebeuf	3·03	2·45	2·30	7·10	7·00	6·20
Villequier	4·00	3·40	3·25	7·40	7·30	6·40
Caudebec	4·15	3·50	3·15	8·00	7·50	7·00
La Mailleraye	4·30	4·15	4·00	8·30	8·20	8·10
Duclair	5·15	5·05	4·45	9·00	9·00	9·25
La Bouille	5·50	5·45	5·40	10·00	10·00	10·00
Rouen	6·25	6·40	6·15	10·50	10·40	10·40

For large ships the calculations of heights in the river are of the greatest importance but for yachtsmen the depths are less necessary and the tidal streams of much more importance. However, knowledge of the behaviour of shipping in the Seine is desirable in order to understand why there is a concentration of shipping at certain times, and not at others.

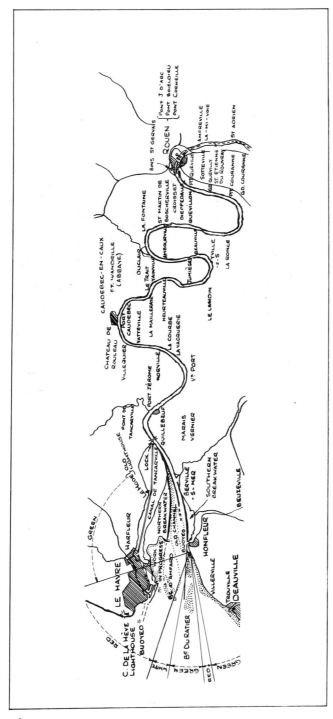

Large ships follow the general rule:

Up river

Leave Le Havre between 4½ hours before HW Le Havre until about 1 hour after HW Le Havre (the latter is applicable for ships doing 13 knots or over).

Down river

Leave Rouen between HW Rouen to LW Le Havre (as already explained, this covers a relatively small period of time).

The foregoing concerning large ships must not be taken too literally since vessels *on passage* will not wait for the tide.

Yachts should therefore set out from Le Havre about 6 hours before HW: they will then have two or three hours during which they will be relatively undisturbed, after which large ships will come belting past and by the time they are well ahead the yachts will be again undisturbed and remain so until they reach Rouen.

To go *down river* yachts should set out about 4½ hours after HW Le Havre, and the same situation will be experienced.

Bad visibility

Bad visibility is a more frequent occurrence, unfortunately even in the summer months, than might be imagined. The months of March and September give clear nights up until midnight but from Villequier up-river the remaining hours of darkness are frequently

28. Yachts lying on pontoon in the Bassin St Gervais, Rouen.

accompanied by fog. The test which all the pilots apply is to run the hand down the outside of the wheelhouse—if it is wet then fog is on the way. It is therefore very necessary to moor or anchor as soon as possible. An important note on mooring is that yachts should not moor at the side of a barge or pontoon because the wash from shipping will cause rolling, with resulting damage to topsides. The advice is, therefore, to moor fore and aft.

All shipping will exercise greater care and proceed with radar, observing that every ship (above 50 tons) will have a pilot on board. For a yacht the difficulty is to choose a suitable place, so the following has been drawn up with the help of the pilots, together with some notes on the countryside.

Station 338*   At Tancarville, just the other side of the bridge on the port side moor between any two of the barges waiting to go through the Tancarville lock, or between piles if these are unoccupied (but be ready to slip if barges arrive). There are also some small mooring buoys a little further up.

331   Quillebeuf, quite a nice looking place, which starts a change of scenery and the countryside becomes more wooded. Mooring buoys.

*338 refers to the distance from Paris in kilometres. There are many tide gauges, and from La Mailleraye upwards many of them display this figure, which is very helpful in establishing precise whereabouts. The distance is also painted in yellow on the embankment in certain places.

A plan of the river showing kilometre markings will be found most useful: see note 10 in the appendix (p. 123).

327	At Corvette, on the starboard hand, is a section of Mulberry Harbour from Arromanches.
323	The village of Azier on the starboard hand has a fine 11th century tower.
314	Villequier is where pilots are changed; consequently all ships go dead slow and, therefore, a good place to moor is on the port side near the pilot station.
310	Caudebec-en-Caux—a really beautiful small town. There is a sailing school (Ecole de Voile du T.C.F.). Several small yacht moorings.
308	The seaplane carved in the cliff face commemorates the attempted rescue of Amundsen.
306–304	Do not anchor on the port hand side as there is insufficient depth of water.
303–302	La Mailleraye. Excellent anchorage. There is adequate depth for yachts, but insufficient for large craft. Do not use the mooring buoys.
300–299	Anchorage is possible at either end near the dolphins on the starboard hand.
294–293	Do not anchor at Trondes Hogues, as it dries.
283–291	Good anchorage close to the bank of the starboard side.
278	At Duclair mooring is quite alright at the wharf on the port side, if it is free, or anchoring on the opposite side just before or just beyond the ferry.
276–275	At Berville the Yacht Club CVSM (Cercle de la Voile de la Seine Maritime) has moorings for very small craft (up to 3 ft draft). There is a small pontoon suitable for mooring dinghies outside the Club House, which is suitable for a short call.
274–273	On the starboard side opposite the fixed red light with 'd'Henouville' painted on it there is a good anchorage.
273–272	On the port hand side between 273–272 is St Georges Yachting Club, but anchoring opposite is better.
269	On the starboard hand on the hill is a castle known as Le Corset Rouge and the story goes that when the Lord of the manor used to go away from time to time to fight in the Crusades his lady hung her corsets out of her window to indicate to a monk living on the other side at St-Martin-de-Boscherville that the coast was clear, so to speak. This arrangement eventually miscarried when her husband returned unexpectedly; he promptly despatched the monk with his sword, dipped the corsets in the blood and draped them from the window for all to see!
260	The ruins of Robert the Devil's castle, father of William the Conqueror. Moor to buoys or anchor. There are numerous good restaurants here.
255	On the port hand is the Colonne Napoleon. This is to commemorate the place where Napoleon's body was laid in order to satisfy his request to be buried on the banks of the Seine. Subsequently his body was taken by a horse-drawn barge to Les Invalides in Paris.
254	From this station until arrival at Rouen at 243 there is nowhere suitable to moor or anchor.

Rouen

It is advisable to be abeam of Honfleur no later than 4 hours before HW Le Havre. There is always sufficient water for yachts in the channel. The tide floods at up to 5 knots, a considerable help. But beware strong eddies in places, which makes use of autopilots unadvisable. It is forbidden to steer to port or to cross over the channel, under sail or power. Various tugs, motor barges and ferries will be encountered and despite the skill of the Seine pilots collisions are not unusual. Except in fog, an overnight stop is usually unadvisable, there being a scarcity of buoys or wharfs for mooring, and the bottom too muddy for safe anchoring. There is also the danger of running aground at low tide or being damaged against a wharf or pontoon by the wash from passing traffic. At spring tides there is still a residual bore: before dredging reduced it, the original *mascaret* at Villequier sank a boat carrying Victor Hugo's daughter and her husband, drowning them both, and the poet's statue can be seen on the northern bank, gazing sorrowfully at the scene of the disaster.

At Rouen, the harbour and entrance to the Bassins Saint Gervais are the first opening on the port hand. Here it is possible to moor to a small pontoon well in along the south side, but without facilities for yachts. One km further is the harbourmaster's office, where you must stop. A crane for dismasting can be hired by phone from here. Even better, moor in the Bassin St Gervais, and ring the Brothers Villetard ((35) 88-00-00), who are always extremely helpful. Avoid mooring alongside the quay, because of the continuous movement of shipping. Once the mast is out, having passed the statues and bridges of William the Conqueror, Joan of Arc, Boieldieu and Pierre Corneille, one finds the Port Fluvial, on the north bank of the Ile Lacroix. Water and fuel are available on the Villetard Bros. pontoons, and the mooring is a comfortable one as through traffic passes the other side of the island. Fast trains to Paris—one hour. However visitors not intending to go higher up the river are unlikely to go to the expense of dismasting just to visit this berth, when it is possible to lie below the bridges, although it is a good half-hour's walk from the St Gervais berth to the centre of Rouen.

Note: It is expressly forbidden for pleasure craft to navigate at night between Rouen and Cap du Hode, which lies just upstream from Honfleur. Those with VHF should also note that for link calls Rouen Radio must be called up on Channel 25 or 27, not 16. Port Control operates on Channel 11.

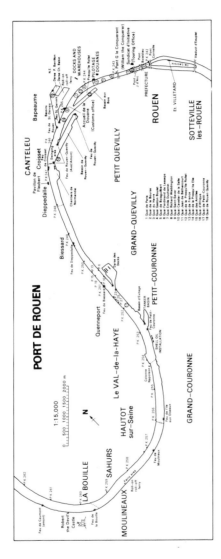

Plan 14 Port of Rouen showing the site of the new Yacht Club on Ile Lacroix.

Notes

It is not intended to provide in this book an exhaustive treatise covering the Le Havre–Rouen passage, or to make any observations on the further passage to Paris and beyond. For fuller details, the *Guide to the French Inland Waterways*, published and regularly revised by the Cruising Association, Ivory House, St. Katharine Dock, London E1 9AT will be found useful, as also *La Mer*, referred to above, and the *Channel Pilot*. It only remains to add that mosquitoes can be troublesome, and it is wise to be equipped with an effective repellant.

Honfleur

Charts Nos. 2613 and 2146

This twelfth century town is another port which has seen much strife over the years, but its only permanent enemy is the mud. It was taken by the English at one time, but given back to the French by the Treaty of Brittany. Until the fifteenth century it has a strong military flavour though the only remaining evidence of this is La Lieutenance, a marvellous building just to the west of the lock into the yacht basin, which houses the Capitainerie. For two hundred years there were strong ties with Canada and America; in 1608 Samuel de Champlain sailed from Honfleur to found the province of Quebec. There is one of the most interesting churches in the whole of Normandy (Eglise St Catherine), and yachtsmen should certainly look at it: clearly this

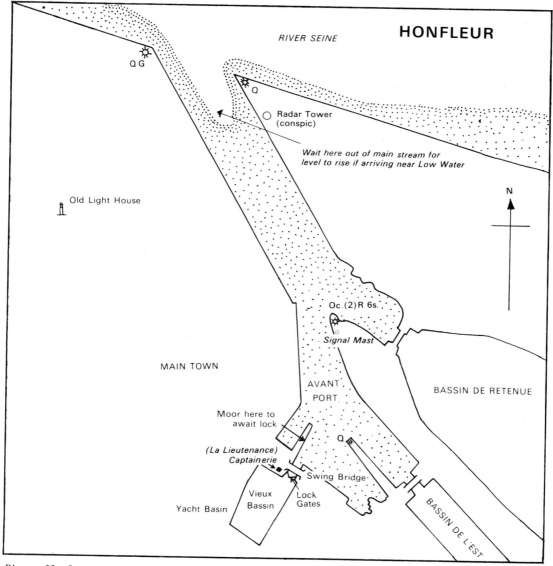

Plan 15 Honfleur.

29. Honfleur: entrance channel showing radar tower.

15th century church, built entirely of wood, was made by shipwrights. The steeple belfry, incidentally, is not on top of the tower but stands a little to the side of the main part of the church.

Local yachtsmen are surprisingly critical of this charming harbour and say it is dirty; the author and his family who have frequently visited it do not subscribe to this, but find it extremely pleasant and restful. It is much frequented by artists, not surprisingly as it is so picturesque. There is no yacht club, which partly contributes to the feeling of being away from it all, but it is a most interesting mediaeval town with excellent restaurants.

Approach
The vast majority will be approaching from down river, in which case there should be few problems. The well-buoyed channel is followed as far as starboard buoy 19, and almost at once the narrow harbour entrance opens up on the starboard hand. If the flood is still strong, one must take care not to be swept past the entrance, at night keeping the Oc (2) R light at the inner end of the entrance channel midway between the entrance lights (QG and Q) until safely in the channel. There is a lighthouse on the Falaise des Fonds, about a mile W of the entrance, showing Fl (3) 12s., R. downstream and G. upstream, but this is of little help in my experience. By day, the entrance can be recognised for miles by the elegant white radar tower, with an observation gallery projecting northwards near the top, which stands on the east side of the entrance channel.

Notes on the timing of the approach from Le Havre or Deauville will be found under Seine

62

30. Honfleur: the Avant Port is to the right of the signal mast.

Pilotage on page 54. If it is decided to spend a night at Honfleur after making the passage down the Seine, however, a few additional notes may be useful. Coming down the river on the full ebb, the radar tower becomes an invaluable mark, as the entrance is invisible from the east until you are almost past it, and if you overshoot it can take a long time to claw your way back up against the tide, which runs very strongly. The entrance channel dries at LWS, but fortunately there is plenty of water—at least 2 m—extending far enough in to bring one out of the tidal stream of the Seine, into a gentle ebb stream from the harbour. In these circumstances, press boldly up the middle of the channel (there are obstructions near the edges) and put her aground on soft mud, where you may lie comfortably until the new flood enables you first to enter the Avant Port, and later the Vieux Bassin. In spite of constant plans to dredge it, the Avant Port also dries almost wholly at LWS.

Berthing

To await the opening of the lock or bridge, the best place to lie is close to the bridge, on the east side of the mole which projects from the shore just west of the bridge (see plan). However, if arriving after the lock has closed with a view to taking the ground, only the northern half of the mole is safe, as there is a concrete sill near the bridge. Even here, the ground slopes steeply away from the mole, so bilge-keelers take up an awkward angle. The lock opens from one hour before to two hours after high water, and the bridge opens at −1, HW, +1, and +2, except at night (0001–0600) when the +2 opening is omitted. On entering the wet basin, moor as space allows, bows on and stern to a buoy.

63

31. Honfleur: entrance to the yacht basin is just behind the mole. The Lieutenance is at the right of the picture.

32. Honfleur: yachts in the Vieux-Bassin.

64

The tides

There are certain freak characteristics of the tide which should be mentioned, and to some extent they compensate for Honfleur's built-in enemy, the mud. There is in effect a double high water. The flood runs for $4\frac{1}{2}$ hours, after which the tide remains slack for a couple of hours before the ebb begins. Resulting from the tidal behaviour both at Honfleur and at Trouville it is possible to leave the yacht basin at Honfleur at the beginning of high water and arrive at Trouville at the end of it; and still be in plenty of time to enter the old harbour.

Although Honfleur is not a large or important yacht harbour, there is an excellent shipyard that can undertake repairs: Société Nouvelle des Ateliers et Chantiers Maritime on the E jetty (Tel. (31) 89-13-71). They have a first class team of carpenters. The Renault garage, 14 Quai Lepaulmier (Tel. 89-18-67) will undertake engine repairs. Other useful addresses are the Customs, Quai Lepaulmier (Tel. 89-12-13), and the Capitainerie (Tel. 89-20-02). They also have VHF Channel 11. For tidal streams see pages 52 and 53.

Deauville and Trouville

Charts Nos. 2613 and 2146

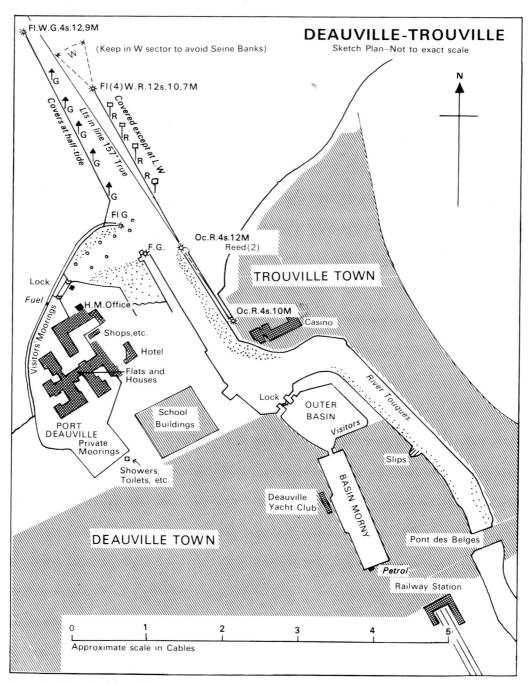

Fl.W.G.4s.12,9M

(Keep in W sector to avoid Seine Banks)

DEAUVILLE–TROUVILLE

Sketch Plan–Not to exact scale

N

Fl(4)W.R.12s.10,7M

Covered except at L.W

Covers at half-tide

Lts in line 157° True

G G G G G G G

R R R R R R

Fl G

F.G.

Oc.R.4s.12M
Reed(2)

TROUVILLE TOWN

Lock

Fuel

H.M.Office

Visitors' Moorings

Shops,etc.

Hotel

Flats and Houses

Oc.R.4s.10M

Casino

Lock

OUTER BASIN

Visitors

River Touques

School Buildings

PORT DEAUVILLE

Private Moorings

Showers, Toilets, etc.

Slips

Deauville Yacht Club

BASIN MORNY

Pont des Belges

DEAUVILLE TOWN

Petrol

Railway Station

| 0 | 1 | 2 | 3 | 4 | 5 |

Approximate scale in Cables

Plan 16   Deauville–Trouville.

Deauville is one of the great Victorian watering-places which has survived into a dignified old age, still magnificent and grandiose if a little shabby in places. The yacht club is large and welcoming, there are rival Casinos, a busy racecourse, and more restaurants to the square mile than anywhere I have ever been. The great shops and restaurants cater for the wealthy visitors who still come every season, but there are numerous cafés and restaurants where the prices are modest and good value for money is offered as long as the visitor is prepared to step a few yards off the main boulevards.

Approach and Entrance

The approach should be from due N through to W but not from E of N because of the Banc du Ratier. The most conspicuous building is the casino at Trouville. There is an E Cardinal buoy, VQ (3) 5s, which it is desirable to identify if possible. This buoy lies $2\frac{1}{2}$ miles from the harbour entrance and is almost in transit with the leading marks. It is very helpful to be able to pass it close abeam and to starboard and thus to establish position and course.

From this position, one can steer straight for the pierheads on about 160° (mag.). An unlit west cardinal bell-buoy, Trouville SW, will be seen about $\frac{3}{4}$ mile to starboard about a mile before the pierheads are reached. Coming from the west, if an offing of around $1\frac{1}{2}$ miles is maintained, course may be altered for the entrance when this buoy is reached.

At night there are no problems. The white sectors of the two outer lights provide a safe angle of approach, and when closer in the leading lights (Oc R 4s), will be visible, and provide a safe line through the outer pierheads. It should be noted however that the front light is obscured from anywhere on the northeast side of the line of the eastern outer breakwater, and the rear one can not be seen from much west of the line, so the two are seen together only when close to the line.

The approach and entrance is not hazardous even for a stranger and at night, provided the weather is reasonable. With strong winds between west and north, however, the place is best avoided except by those with local knowledge. In such conditions the approach should be made during the period from two hours before to high water, but in good weather and with moderate draft the harbour is available at all times except about $2\frac{1}{2}$ hours either side of low water.

The approach course is only critical close in and near low water, when the sunken extension of the east pier becomes a hazard, but as long as the last part of the approach is made along the line of the inner piers (or leading lights at night), there are no problems. Keep outside the posts marking the shoals off the end of the curved outer W breakwater.

Berthing

At this point, if not before, the choice between Port Deauville and the old harbour of Deauville-Trouville has to be made. The great advantage of the former is that it is available for longer: indeed the locks will operate at any time a vessel can succeed in reaching them afloat. The channel dries out up to $1\frac{1}{2}$ metres in summer, which means in practice that yachts drawing up to $1\frac{1}{2}$ metres can get in and out all but 2 hours each side of low water neaps, or $2\frac{1}{2}$ hours of low water at springs. This is of course assuming moderate weather for the approach. The old harbour, on the other hand, has lock gates which open for only $4\frac{1}{2}$ hours every tide. It is, however, materially cheaper, and the moorings are far more convenient for shopping and access to the town.

33. Deauville: the W outer light at right of picture. Follow the starboard beacons and turn to starboard before the inner entrance for Port Deauville, straight on for the Vieux Port.

Port Deauville

To enter, turn to starboard round the outer breakwater, leaving black posts to starboard, and red posts or buoys to port. The lock opens on demand, and operates very quickly: the author averaged ten minutes in 1982. Visitors' moorings are along the inside of the main breakwater to starboard, on individual pontoons (the first part without pontoons being for large sail training vessels and the like).

The visitors moorings are conveniently situated for the facilities of the port, all of which can now be reached by a short walk by way of a footbridge over the lock. (Before this bridge was built, one could only reach the Port Office and other facilities by walking round the whole harbour, or launching the dinghy and rowing across.) Facilities include fuel (just inside the locks on the north side: not available near HW when both lock gates are left open: no charge for locking in to fuel), a 45-ton lift, 15-ton crane, chandlery, restaurants and hotel (expensive even by local standards); water on the pontoons.

The real snag about Port Deauville are the charges, which are very high compared with other ports in the area, including the Vieux Port of Deauville-Trouville. For example, in high season (July-August) 1982, one night for a boat 8–9m LOA cost 79 francs at Port Deaville, and only 32 francs in the Vieux Port. It is also much further from the town and beaches, although it is possible to ask for a berth in the southern part of the harbour, which removes this disadvantage.

68

34. Deauville: entrance to the Old Harbour, taken from the head of the outer breakwater near low water.

35. Deauville: Old Yacht Harbour.

The Old Harbour of Deauville-Trouville

This is normally referred to as Le Vieux Port to distinguish it from the new harbour at Port Deauville. To enter, having passed the outer breakwater, leave the western inner pierhead close to starboard, and proceed down the starboard side of the channel, as the best water lies about one third of the distance from the west pier to the east.

The lock gates open from 2 hours before high water Deauville to 2½ hours after. The time of HW Deauville varies considerably from the approximation given in Reed's. Very roughly, for tidal heights below 7·0 m it is 20 minutes before HW Le Havre; from 7·1 to 7·5 is 30–40 minutes before, and over 7·5 m it can be as much as 1 hour 10 minutes before HW Le Havre. Deauville Y.C. will send an accurate tide table on request.

Once through the lock, the visitors' pontoon will be found on the wall E of the swing bridge opposite. Large yachts (over 14 m) anchor NW of this pontoon and secure stern to the quay. The yacht club is large and friendly, with good showers and toilet facilities, and an excellent bar. Petrol (only) by hose from the filling station at the south end of the Bassin Morny. Diesel can be bought there but only in cans. Water by hose. The modest harbour dues will be collected by the club, to whom visitors should report as soon as possible after arrival. Useful telephone numbers include: Yacht Club: (secretariat, office hours only) (31) 88-38-19; bar (manned during waking hours!) 88-38-00; Capitainerie: 88-28-71; Customs: 88-35-29; Capitainerie Port Deauville: 88-56-16 or 88-24-20; Chantiers de la Touques (repairs to hull, motor etc.): 88-05-75.

Tidal information

HEIGHT ABOVE DATUM OF SOUNDINGS IN METRES

High water		Low water	
Mean springs	Mean neaps	Mean springs	Mean neaps
7·7	6·3	0·8	2·5

The west-going stream begins at HW Dover − 1, the east-going at HW Dover − 6. Rates attain 1.5 knots at mean springs.

River Dives, Cabourg and Houlgate

Charts Nos. 2613 and 1821

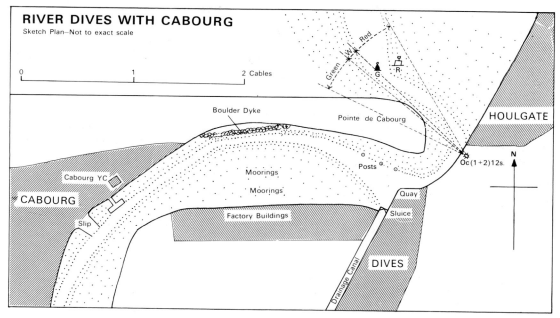

Plan 17   River Dives with Cabourg.

When William the Conqueror assembled his fleet in the River Dives before the invasion of England, it formed a major port in this part of Normandy. Today there would be no room for the 400 ships and 1000 transports that are said to have made up the fleet, but there remain a few fishing boats and a substantial fleet of shallow draft local yachts in the much silted river. The haven has great charm, but should only be visited by a boat prepared to dry without support, and after prior arrangement with the YC at Cabourg.

The streams are not strong, but it is important to assess the time of HW accurately. From my observations, the tide turns at Cabourg about 15 minutes before HW Le Havre at springs, and some 30 minutes earlier at neaps. At the entrance the turn is about 45 minutes earlier in both cases.

71

36. Dives: fishing boat wharf and entrance near LW.

37. Cabourg: the yacht club jetty at a lowish high water. The harbourmaster, M. Hervé, is in the foreground.

72

When coming from either the east or the west, the entrance to the river can be judged by the gap between Houlgate and Cabourg. The shore should then be closed to about a mile, keeping the sounder going, by which time the offing buoys should have been located. As shown on the plan, these consist of a green conical buoy to be left to starboard and a red can buoy to be left to port. The positions of these buoys are changed periodically to take account of shifts in the channel.

The channel always keeps very close along the eastern side of the entrance, the best water being only a few metres from the shingle, which makes it rather reminiscent of the Deben. Once inside, one can tie up for a short time at the quay at Dives: for a longer visit, proceed along the channel to Cabourg. From Dives quay this cuts across towards the N bank, unmarked except for a few posts marking rocks off the beach (all to be left to starboard) and by the fact that it is clear of moorings. On a spring tide in 1982, there was a minimum depth of 3 metres between the entrance and the YC staging at Cabourg.

If planning to stay more than a tide, it is wiser to telephone the harbourmaster at Cabourg YC, Tel. (31) 91-23-55), to make sure that there will be room alongside on the jetty, or a buoy available. The bottom is flat, mud and pebbles, so one can safely take the ground alongside in a bilge-keeler, or with a keel with suitable precautions. The club, rebuilt in 1976, is charming, with an unusual clinker-built bar. No other facilities, but a good bathing beach north of the town, on the seaward side of the point.

Tidal information

HEIGHT ABOVE DATUM OF SOUNDINGS IN METRES

High water		Low Water	
Mean springs	Mean neaps	Mean springs	Mean neaps
7·4	6·0	0·7	2·3

Tidal streams are similar to those off Deauville.

Ouistreham

Charts Nos. 2613 and 1821

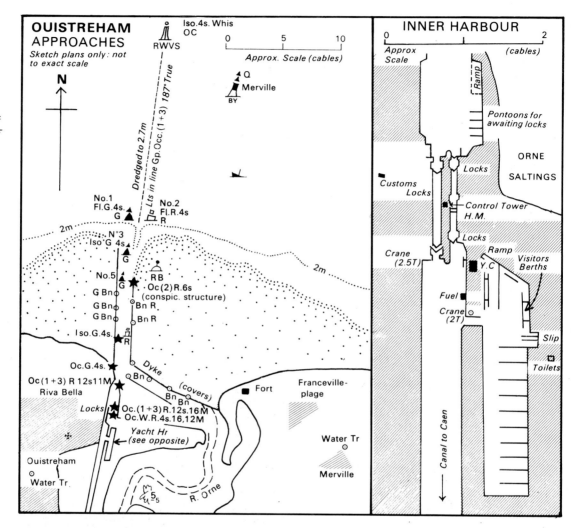

Plan 18 Ouistreham: approaches and inner harbour.

The only really good deep harbour between Le Havre and Cherbourg is Ouistreham. Deep draft steamships cannot enter at low water since the channel is dredged only to 2·7 m but yachts can enter at any state of tide up to the locks at the end of the Avant Port. Dredgers are constantly at work in the channel. However, it may be wise not to enter at dead low water springs in strong onshore winds.

74

Ouistreham is sited at the mouth of the river Orne and the seaward end of the Caen Canal and, although there is a fair quantity of commercial traffic up and down the canal, it does not in fact qualify as a big commercial port, nor indeed does it come into the category of an important fishing port but preserves a balance between commerce, fishing and yachting.

Approaches

Whether making a landfall from the east or the west the main lighthouse is probably the most easily visible landmark, followed by the built-up seaside resort of Riva Bella on the western side of the entrance. About three miles seaward of the lighthouse and in line with the leading marks is the main Ouistreham buoy. It is a RWVS pillar buoy, Iso. 4 secs., fitted with a whistle, and is marked O.C.

The course from this buoy is 192° (mag.) to a pair of buoys, No. 1, G, Fl. G. 4s, and No. 2, R, Fl. R 4s. It is now important not to depart too far from the course of 192°. The tide sets roughly E and W and although never stronger than a knot and a half this may be enough to upset calculations.

The first pair of buoys marks the start of the dredged channel; soon after leaving them behind the sunken breakwaters begin; there are beacons placed at irregular intervals on them. The ends of the sunken breakwaters are marked by light beacons: Oc G 4s on the starboard (W) side and Oc (2) R 6s on the port. Next comes a starboard light structure, Oc (1 + 3) R 12 S, the front one of the two synchronised leading lights. When nearly abeam of this structure keep to the western or starboard hand side of the channel since the best water is on this side. The new, large lock to the west and the older smaller one on the east are now dead ahead. The description sounds complicated, but in fact

38. Ouistreham: the lighthouse, leading lights and control tower.

39. Ouistreham: moorings and the control tower. Small lock to the left of the control tower, large lock to the right. The after leading light is to the left of the lighthouse.

leaving red to port and green to starboard in daylight, or using the leading lights after dark, makes the entry perfectly simple.

There are pontoons just before the locks on the port side of the channel where one can wait for the locks to open, but it is not advisable to stay any longer than necessary, or leave a boat unattended there, as there can be considerable wash from passing traffic.

The locks operate from two hours before until $2\frac{1}{4}$ hours after high water except in July and August, when the opening times are extended to 3 hours before to $3\frac{1}{4}$ hours after. The lock will operate at the beginning and end of the period, and as often between as traffic warrants. It is wise to arrive at least half an hour before the last opening, as the locks work slowly.

The main lighthouse, white with a red band round the top part, has a characteristic of Oc WR 4s, and just in front of it is the rear leading light, Oc $(1 + 3)$ R 12s, which is synchronised with the front leading light.

The foregoing covers the channel, both by day and by night, and no difficulty should be experienced in negotiating it. Incidentally the River Orne has a fair number of small yachts at mooring and a clubhouse (Yacht Club de la Baie de l'Orne), but the moorings are not to be recommended except for twin bilge keel or multi-hull craft and it is rather exposed to winds from all points of the compass. Visitors should therefore lock in and use the yacht basin on the E side of the canal just inside the lock.

The yacht club at Ouistreham is at the NW corner of the yacht basin. Fuel can be obtained from a jetty on the port side after coming out of the lock towards Caen. General information and advice can be obtained from the President of the club, Société des Regates de Caen–Ouistreham

(Tel. (31) 97-13-05). The Club is open from 0900–1200 and 1400–1800, and collects dues for the yacht berths. Showers, toilets etc, are available: the former in opening hours only, the latter at all times. The main shopping centre of the town is quite close to the locks but a little hard to find. It lies WSW of the locks, clustered round the large church. Excellent shops and restaurants.

Other names and addresses are:

Capitainerie (31) 97-14-43 (also listens on Channel 16, working channels 12 or 68).
Hull repairs: Serra Marine, on the yacht basin (97-03-60), or Nauti-Plaisance (97-03-08).
Engine repairs: Lemels, Quai Charcot, on starboard side of canal just inside the lock (96-21-91), or Nauti-Plaisance as above.

The Caen Canal

From the locks at Ouistreham to Caen is about 16 km, roughly 8 nautical miles. In daytime in summer there is one series of free bridge openings in each direction, timed for boats leaving the first bridge above Ouistreham at 1930, and for boats leaving Caen at 0835. Otherwise, yachts wishing to make the passage should call at the office in the lock control tower and see if there is a commercial vessel scheduled to use the canal. If so, the yacht will be allowed to accompany it (on payment of dues) but the bridges are no longer opened for unaccompanied yachts. There is a yacht harbour at the east end of the Bassin St Pierre in Caen, near the centre of the city: showers, toilets and all facilities. Charts available at Voilerie Patrice Quesnel, 22 ave du 6 Juin, Tel. (31) 85-70-36.

Tidal information

HEIGHT ABOVE DATUM OF SOUNDINGS IN METRES

High water		Low water	
Mean springs	Mean neaps	Mean springs	Mean neaps
7·5	6·1	0·7	2·5

The west-going stream off Ouistreham starts at HW Dover $-\frac{1}{2}$, and attains a peak rate of 1·5 knots (mean springs) at HW Dover $+2$. The east-going stream starts at HW Dover -6, and reaches a peak of 1·8 knots at HW Dover -5.

Courseulles-sur-Mer

Charts Nos. 2613, 1821, and 2073

This, like many other ports along this coast, is a drying harbour and it should be avoided in bad weather, particularly in winds Force 6 and over from the W through N to the NE. It was part of the invasion coast during the last war and it was here that General de Gaulle landed with the Free French contingent in June 1944.

Except in the conditions warned against in the opening paragraph Courseulles is an attractive yachting harbour and in the summer months the wet basins are filled with yachts, many of them large and drawing up to 2 m.

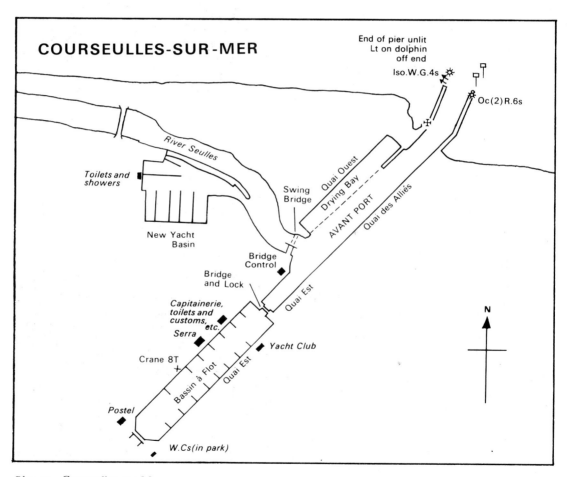

Plan 19   Courseulles-sur-Mer

40. Courseulles: harbour entrance.

41. Courseulles: the entrance channel looking towards the lock.

The harbour is 24 miles west of Le Havre and 39 miles east of Cape Barfleur; it is slightly east of Arromanches, where the Allies built a deep water harbour for the D day landings in the course of a few days. In good weather, Arromanches is worth a visit, and provides a sheltered anchorage, with its hazards either removed or buoyed. But it is unlit, and should not be attempted at night.

The identification of Courseulles from offshore is much aided by the spires of the churches of Langrune, St. Aubin and Bernieres. These are marked on the chart, and from seaward appear to stand in a straight line at exactly regular intervals. The harbour entrance will be found an identical distance to the westward as that between either pair of adjacent churches. Note that although there is a church at Courseulles, and it is marked on the chart, it is quite invisible from any distance to seaward.

In daytime, do not expect to use Pte de Ver lighthouse, $2\frac{1}{4}$ miles W of Courseulles, as a landmark. Although the light is 42m above sea level, it is totally inconspicuous as the height is provided by the land, and the tower itself is squat, undistinguished, and stands among other buildings. In poor visibility, however, the radio beacon is useful. This has a range of 20 miles, and transmits ÉR (··—·· ·—·) on 291.9 kHz. At night, the light (Fl (3) 15s) is visible for 26 miles.

Approach

The harbour entrance dries, and one should not attempt to enter or leave except within 2 hours of local HW, which HW Le Havre – 30 minutes (and not as published elsewhere: this figure comes from the lockmaster at the harbour, and he should know!). In strong onshore winds arrival or departure should be confined to one hour either side of HW: in really calm weather it is possible with draft under 4 feet to scrape in $2\frac{1}{2}$ hours before or after, but this should only be attempted in ideal conditions, with no swell. At night, approach with the W sector of the WG light off the W pier in line with the Oc (2) R 6s light on the E pierhead: leave the former to starboard, and then steer for the latter and leave it to port. Keep close in to the east pier until past the wooden section, as the west side is shoal. In daylight, the large black dolphin off the end of the west pier is now the most conspicuous mark, and will probably be identified before the white light tower on the east one. Having identified these, approach on a course of about 205° (mag.) until close in, when you should keep to the port (E) side of the channel until the end of the wooden part of the east pier, after which the best water is to be found in the middle. Once inside, the lock gates for the old basin will be found dead ahead: the new basin lies up a channel on the starboard side, through a swing bridge. This lies just beyond the drying ramp on the NW side of the channel.

Berthing

The lock gates open from 2 hours before to 2 hours after HW. The basin inside the lock is more convenient than the new basin, but the latter, which has no gates but is protected by a sill, has the advantage that for draft up to 1·20 m, it is available $2\frac{1}{2}$ hours either side of high water. This can be useful in calm weather if one has just missed the lock gates, or wishes to leave as early as

42. Courseulles: half-way up channel. There are temporary moorings outside the lock.

43. Courseulles: the yacht basin taken from the bridge. The lock is at the centre of the picture.

possible the following day. Toilets and showers at the NW end of the basin. Both bridges open on demand.

In the old basin the first three pontoons on the NW side belong to the Yacht Club (S.R. de Courseulles), to whom the dues are payable: those for the other berths are paid (at the same rate) to the harbourmaster/lock-keeper. Take a free berth (bow to pontoon, stern to buoy) and then report to club or bridge office as appropriate for confirmation. The YC (open 10-1 and 4-8) welcomes visitors. All stores, restaurants etc., in the town, E of the harbour: some restaurants also around the new basin. Water on the pontoons in both basins.

Useful positions and telephone numbers are:

Repairs and Chandlery: Serra Marine, Quai Ouest, Tel. (31) 97-42-34.
Repairs and Shipwrights: Postel et Cie., Quai Ouest, Tel (31) 97-45-08.
Yacht Club: Tel. (31) 97-47-42.
Berth Reservations: M. Jean of Ponts et Chaussees, Tel. (31) 97-46-03.
Capitainerie: Quai Ouest.

Tidal information
Range of tide at Mean springs: 7·3 metres; at Mean neaps: 2·6 metres.
For tidal streams see under Ouistreham.

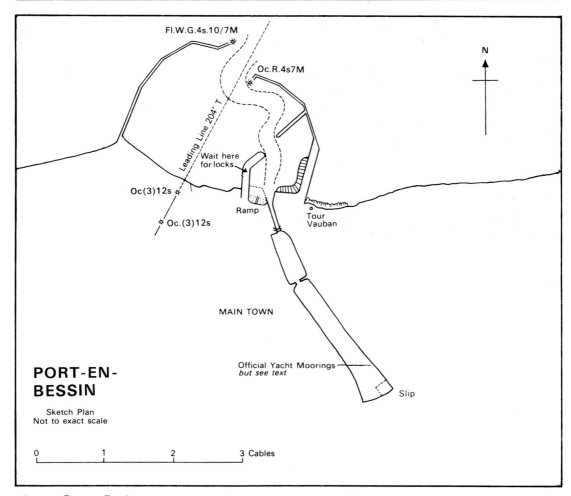

FI.W.G.4s.10/7M

Oc.R.4s7M

N

Leading Line 204° T

Wait here for locks

Oc(3)12s

Oc.(3)12s

Ramp

Tour Vauban

MAIN TOWN

Official Yacht Moorings
but see text

Slip

PORT-EN-BESSIN

Sketch Plan
Not to exact scale

0   1   2   3 Cables

Plan 20   Port-en-Bessin.

This little fishing port has no real provision for yachts, but it is a charming town. One must be prepared to lie alongside a fishing boat, and they are not all terribly cooperative. Getting ashore can require some athletic ability.

The entrance can be rough in winds from between N and NE, and indeed in winds of force 6 and over in this quarter, entrance should not be attempted.

There is little room for yachts in the drying harbour outside the wet basin—the best place to lie while awaiting the lock gates is as shown on the plan: on the eastern side of the mole which forms the west wall of the inner harbour. Keep to the northern half of this, to avoid the concrete

44. Port-en-Bessin: harbour entrance.

45. Port-en-Bessin: a fishing trawler leaving the inner basin.

84

careening ramp at the south end: the extent of this is marked by a painted strip on the top of the wall.

The harbour should only be approached at more than half tide: the gates to the inner dock open two hours either side of high water, during which time the bridge opens for five minutes every whole and half hour.

46. Port-en-Bessin.

Entrance and Berthing

The entrance to the harbour is comparatively easy. At night the two leading lights are Oc (3) 12s, on 204° True. By day, the upper one is on the side of a house, and the lower one on an iron structure painted white beside a small round white tower which houses the fog siren (one long blast followed by a series of short blasts). There is a radio beacon (BS – ·· ··) on 313·5 kHZ (range 5 miles).

Inside the pierheads, the best water lies in a curved channel which lies as indicated on the plan. However, two hours either side of high water, this is not likely to be critical, and one can safely steer straight for the entrance to the inner harbour with draft up to 2 m. Await the lock gates alongside as described earlier: if too late it is safe to take the ground in good weather, as the bottom is smooth flat mud, but in strong onshore winds there is a dangerous swell, and yachts should on no account remain if the gates have shut.

Once through the locks, proceed into the second (southern) basin and berth alongside a fishing boat as opportunity offers. There is a small space at the far end of the harbour reserved for 'plaisance', but this is almost always occupied by very small local craft, far too small to moor alongside; and in any case the wall there slopes outwards steeply, making it virtually unusable by a seagoing yacht. The harbour tends to be noisy if HW is in the middle of the night, as fishing boats enter and then manoeuvre for several hours thereafter, moving to the fish dock to unload and then back to their berths. The best time for a visit is therefore when HW is around seven or eight o'clock, when one can expect a relatively untroubled night.

Facilities
Although in no way a yacht harbour, there are two wood boat-builders at the S end of the basin, capable of repairs; 4 ton and (mobile) 6 ton cranes; motor repairs from Francoise Digne on the W side of the basin, or Sominex at the S end. Water taps on E quay. Good shops (excellent fish) and restaurants along the W side of the N basin. Buses to Bayeux, home of the famous tapestry, leave several times a day: the journey takes about 25 minutes, and is well worth making.

Tidal information
Range at Mean springs: 6·2 m; at Mean neaps: 3·3 m.
Streams are similar to Ouistreham.

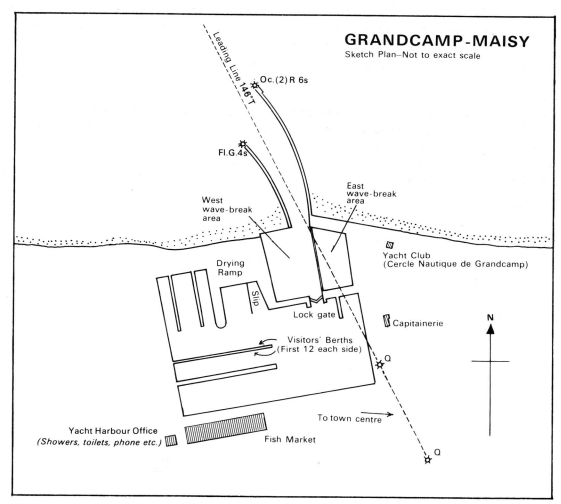

GRANDCAMP-MAISY
Sketch Plan—Not to exact scale

Oc.(2)R 6s

Leading Line 146°T

Fl.G.4s

West
wave-break
area

East
wave-break
area

Drying
Ramp

Slip

Yacht Club
(Cercle Nautique de Grandcamp)

Lock gate

Capitainerie

Visitors' Berths
(First 12 each side)

N

Q

To town centre

Q

Yacht Harbour Office
(Showers, toilets, phone etc.)

Fish Market

Plan 21   Grandcamp-Maisy.

Lying just east of the large and muddy estuary of the rivers Carentan and Vire, Grandcamp has been developed comparatively recently into one of the most useful yacht harbours on this part of the coast. It has a thriving fish market, and nearby there are two interesting Chateaux: du Guesclin and de la Tonnellerie. There is some holiday activity, and therefore a number of restaurants of various grades, mostly offering good value especially in the area of sea-food.

47. Grandcamp–Maisy: harbour entrance from seaward.

48. Grandcamp–Maisy: entrance looking towards the inner basin.

88

49. Grandcamp–Maisy: yacht moorings in inner basin.

Approach and Entry

The approach lies over the Roches de Grandchamp, a flat rocky plateau extending along four miles of coast and running over a mile out to sea. However, the rocky area is almost flat and without sudden peaks, and for boats drawing under six feet approach is safe $2\frac{1}{2}$ hours either side of HW unless a big sea is running, when the margin should be reduced to 2 hours or less. At night, two synchronised Q leading lights make identification and entry easy: during the day one may safely steer in on any course between SE and SW. The town cannot be mistaken, owing to the estuary to its west. On arrival, keep near the middle of the channel between the piers, and the lock gates into the inner harbour will be found straight ahead. There is nowhere very comfortable to wait in the outer harbour, but if the approach has been timed as advised, the gates will be open and one can proceed straight into the inner basin.

Berthing and Facilities

The lock gates open from about 2 hours before to $2\frac{1}{2}$ hours after local high water, but in fact by a curious coincidence the tidal rhythm is such that the lock keepers are able to use the tide table for Dunquerque, of all places. The gates open at low water Dunquerque, and close at high water there. This saves them from having to make the complicated calculation of differences on

Cherbourg (see the warning on this subject in the Introduction), and instead they merely look the times up in the tables for a principal port.

Visitors' berths are the outer 25 on the northernmost of the two main pontoons on the west side of the inner basin. Water and electricity on the pontoons, but the diesel pump on the E quay is for fishermen only. Motor and fibreglass repairs, and chandlery, from Galliot Marine on the Quai Ouest, (Tel. (31) 22-67-02): I can strongly recommend their skill and helpfulness. Harbour office with first class showers and toilets at the SW corner of the basin, Tel. 22-63-16. There is also a small yacht club. Buses to Bayeux, which is well worth a visit to see the famous tapestry: the journey takes about an hour.

Tidal Information

Mean rise (estimates only): springs 6·8 m, neaps 5·5 m.

Offshore, the NW stream begins at HW Dover and reaches a peak of 1.2 knots (mean springs) at HW Dover + 3. The SE stream starts at HW Dover − 6, and reaches a peak of 1.2 knots (mean springs) at HW Dover − 4.

Isigny-sur-Mer

Charts Nos. 2613 and 2073

While Isigny is not in any sense a yachting port, it is a town of some interest which visitors who enjoy exploring shallow channels may well consider worth the trouble of visiting.

50. Isigny-sur-Mer: the channel to Isigny lies to the left of the front leading mark.

Approach and Entrance
(For plan see page 93.)
Identify the RWVS bell-buoy 'IS' which lies about three miles WNW of Grandcamp entrance. This buoy has a spherical topmark, and marks the beginning of the Isigny channel. Turn south and proceed with the sounder operating. The first pair of channel buoys should soon be seen, if indeed they were not already in sight from IS. The channel is fairly straight and closely buoyed, and after about four miles it passes between two sunken breakwaters, marked by beacons. At night there are leading lights, Oc (1 + 2) 12s. When the channel forks, keep to the port hand limb, the River Aure, and this leads after half a mile or so to Isigny. Moor to the pontoon on the west (starboard) side, just beyond the boatbuilders quay. It is also possible to moor further on near the bridge, on the port hand. Berths dry at LW. Good shops.

The best time to arrive at the outer buoy is between three and two hours before high water, which occurs about 50 minutes after Cherbourg at spring tides, and 1 hour 20 minutes after at neaps. The channel carries about three metres at high water neaps.

51. Isigny: pontoon mooring on the west bank. The road bridge is at left of picture.

52. Isigny-sur-Mer: mooring against the eastern bank close to the road bridge.

92

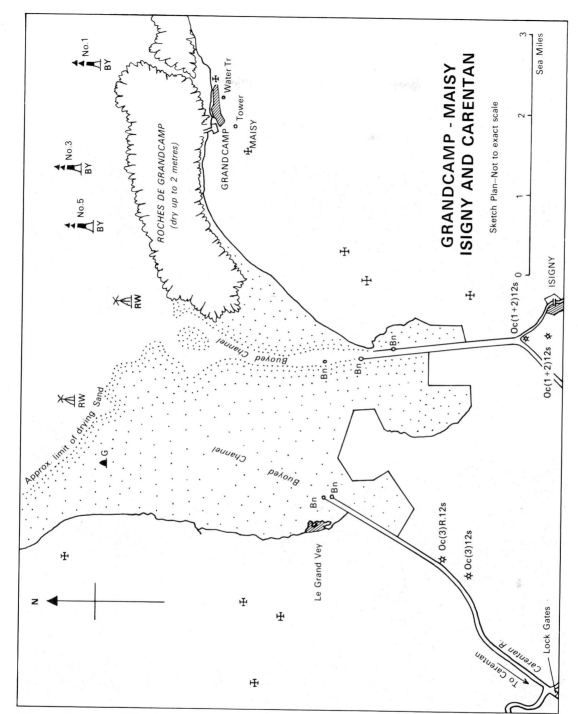

**GRANDCAMP - MAISY
ISIGNY AND CARENTAN**

Sketch Plan—Not to exact scale

No.1
BY

No.3
BY

No.5
BY

ROCHES DE GRANDCAMP
(dry up to 2 metres)

Water Tr

Tower

GRANDCAMP

MAISY

RW

RW

Approx. limit of drying Sand

G

Buoyed Channel

Bn
Bn
Bn

ISIGNY

Oc(1+2)12s

Oc(1+2)12s

Buoyed Channel

Bn
Bn

Le Grand Vey

Oc(3)R.12s

Oc(3)12s

N

Lock Gates

To Carentan

Carentan R.

0   1   2   3
Sea Miles

Plan 22   Grancamp-Maisy, Isigny and Carentan.

53. Carentan Lock: the yacht harbour begins only a couple of hundred yards down the canal.

Carentan has now been developed into a considerable yacht harbour, protected by an efficient lock that ensures a steady water level with 4·5 metres in the yacht harbour. Although it is rather off the direct routes, the town is a pleasant one, and being up a river it has an inland atmosphere, which can make a pleasant change in the middle of a cruise.

Approach and Entry

HW Carentan is about the same as that at Isigny, i.e. 50 minutes after HW Cherbourg at spring tides, and about 1 hour 20 minutes after at neaps. The shallowest part of the approach channel dries about one metre, which means that it has about $2\frac{1}{2}$ metres of water at half tide. It is therefore safe to reach the approach buoy (RW, bell, *CA*) as early as $3\frac{1}{4}$ hours before HW Carentan in light or offshore winds, but in onshore winds it is wiser to delay arrival until 2 hours before. One should not arrive there much after HW Carentan, as it is $7\frac{1}{2}$ miles to the lock gates against a strengthening ebb.

From the approach buoy, which lies 2 miles W of Grandcamp No. 5 buoy, proceed WSW to the first channel buoy, G con with N cone topmark, No. 1, and thence follow the well-marked channel. In 1982, the channel ran almost straight south to the breakwater heads, but it does shift and I have known it describe a wide S shape. The locks will open from HW -2 to $+3$, but they do not operate between 2300 and 0600 except by prior arrangement with the Port Office (Tel. (33) 42-03-55). The buoys have reflective patches, and there are plans to light them, and there are also leading lights (Oc (3) 12s) but these only lead up the inner river. Through the lock, proceed to the yacht pontoons straight ahead and berth as directed. There are 500 berths, so there will probably be plenty of room for a year or two at least.

Facilities

By 1983 there should be showers etc. in the Capitainerie building, and it was hoped that fuel pumps would also be operating. There are already some repair facilities, and these will no doubt build up with the increasing usage of this new development, and I would expect the present lack of chandlery to be rectified too. The town is some 250 metres from the Harbour Office, and offers excellent shopping, banks etc.

Iles St Marcouf

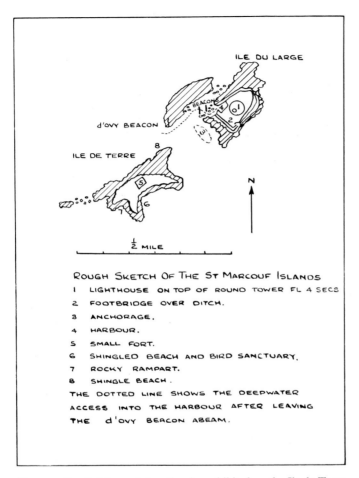

ROUGH SKETCH OF THE ST MARCOUF ISLANDS
1   LIGHTHOUSE ON TOP OF ROUND TOWER FL 4 SECS
2   FOOTBRIDGE OVER DITCH.
3   ANCHORAGE.
4   HARBOUR.
5   SMALL FORT.
6   SHINGLED BEACH AND BIRD SANCTUARY.
7   ROCKY RAMPART.
8   SHINGLE BEACH.
THE DOTTED LINE SHOWS THE DEEPWATER
ACCESS INTO THE HARBOUR AFTER LEAVING
THE d'OVY BEACON ABEAM.

Plan 23   Iles St Marcouf. Landing is prohibited on the Ile de Terre.

These are two fortified islands and were inhabited until 1914: the forts date from the middle of the seventeenth century. Now the only inhabitants are birds, and indeed the Ile de Terre is now an official bird sanctuary and landing there is prohibited. These small islands are but four miles from Utah Beach, one of the invasion sites in 1944.

The lighthouse is on the bigger island, the Ile du Large, and the characteristic of the light is VQ (3) 5s.

54. Iles Saint Marcouf: anchorage is between 'X' and 'X'.

The Iles St Marcouf do not constitute a harbour for yachts but there is an anchorage with a very small harbour for dinghies. The practice which seems to have developed is to sail for a few hours from one of the harbours along the northern shore of the mainland or from Barfleur or St Vaast, drop anchor and then embark in the dinghy for an hour or two ashore, armed with sandwiches and a bottle of wine. During a fine weekend it is not uncommon to count twenty or so dinghies in the tiny harbour.

A visit to the island is not recommended in bad weather, particularly in SW winds, as the anchorage is somewhat exposed.

When arriving at the island for the first time it is prudent to time this at about 2 hours before HW and to leave 2 hours afterwards. This is not on account of the depth of water in the anchorage, since there is plenty at all states of tide, but simply to ensure that the shore-going party will have no difficulty with the dinghy in the harbour.

In the photograph of the beacon it will be seen that the reef to the north is just uncovering, providing a foothold for seagulls. At this state of tide there is about $4\frac{1}{2}$ ft. of water over the rocky ledge into the dinghy harbour.

The anchorage lies approximately SW of the lighthouse and you are strongly urged to anchor at this place and not, for instance, to the NE of the Island because the water is too deep. Some charts show an anchorage to the SE of the Ile de Terre but, as already mentioned, this is now a bird sanctuary. It is possible to land here at certain times of the year, but permission must first be obtained at St. Vaast.

The passage to the islands from St Vaast is quite straightforward and a direct course passes close to a W cardinal buoy, VQ (9) 10s, which marks the SE end of the Banc de la Rade. Between this buoy and the islands the Banc de Saint Marcouf shoals to less than 3 metres, producing bad seas in strong northerly winds.

55. Iles Saint Marcouf: beacon with rocks just awash.

56. Iles Saint Marcouf: dinghy harbour.

To sum up, therefore, the Iles St Marcouf are worth a visit during a fine weekend for fishing and picnicking If solitude is sought, then go during the week out of the holiday season, when the whole place is deserted and there are only the sea birds for company.

St Vaast-la-Hougue

Charts Nos. 2613 and 2073

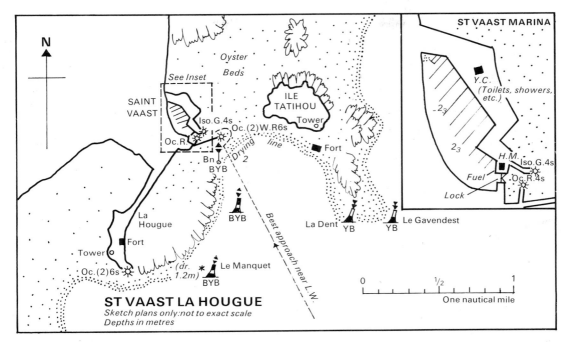

Plan 24   St Vaast-la-Hougue

St Vaast (the final 'st' is mute, leaving it pronounced more or less to rhyme with car) was a main rendezvous for the assembly of William the Conqueror's fleet: rather more recently it was the first French town to be liberated during the Normandy invasion.

This once sleepy little fishing harbour was totally transformed in 1982 by one of the most successful major yachting developments in northern France in recent years. Lock gates were fitted to convert the whole main harbour to a wet basin, the old area of rock-studded mud which made most of the space unusable was dredged out, and pontoon berths for 650 yachts were installed. The space available for the fishing fleet was actually increased, which means that the fishermen are pleased with the development, and are therefore well disposed to the *plaisanciers* in their midst. Available from local HW $-2\frac{1}{2}$ to $+3\frac{1}{2}$ (quarter of an hour less at each end at neaps), this is now the most important yachting centre in the western half of the Baie de la Seine. The harbour is perfectly sheltered in all weathers, but the approach can be difficult in strong E or SE winds, when the least bad conditions will be found within an hour either side of HW.

99

Plan 25 Tower on Tatihou.

Approaches

Coming from the south or east, the Ile de Tatihou must first be identified. This has a conspicuous tower on it (see sketch), but beware of confusing it with a similar one on La Hougue, which is the promontory south of the town of St Vaast. Steer to pass a mile south of Tatihou, leaving the Gavendest and Dent Cardinal S buoys to starboard, after which it is safe to steer straight for the end of the breakwater to the NW.

At night, bring the Oc (2) 6s light on La Hougue into line with the Oc (1 + 3) 12s light at Morsalines, and approach on that line until the breakwater light (Oc (2) WR 6s) bears 325° (mag.), when it is safe to steer for the latter.

From the north, steer to pass at least $\frac{1}{2}$ mile east of Tatihou (which is unmistakable from that quarter) until the Gavendest buoy is identified, when it can be closed. From there, steer west to leave the Dent buoy to starboard, and then NW for the breakwater. At night, this route is complicated by the lack of lights on the Gavendest and Dent buoys , and the light on Pte. de Saire must be kept showing *west* of Barfleur light until the lights on La Hougue and Morsalines come into line, after which proceed as described in the approach from the south.

57. St Vaast-la-Hougue: *La Dent*, south of Ile Tatihou.

58. St Vaast-la-Hougue: the new lock gate and the yacht harbour, still under construction in 1982.

The 'Run' channel is a high tide short cut from Pte. de Saire to the harbour, useful in strong S to W winds, as it avoids the rough seas then found S and E of Tatihou. From 50 m SE of the beacon SE of Pte. de Saire, steer on Quettehou church 267° (mag.) until the cylindrical tower

59. St Vaast-la-Hougue: lighthouse on the end of the outer breakwater. Fishing boat has just turned towards harbour entrance.

60. St Vaast-la-Hougue: view of entrance after rounding the end of the breakwater.

carrying the green light at the north of the entrance appears slightly to seaward of the red light on the south pier. Steer for them keeping them in this relative position, and round the green tower into the harbour. Sound continuously, and do not anchor on this route, as there are oyster beds. The passage can be used with 1·4 m draft from 2 hours before to 1 hour after HW Le Havre.

Entrance and Berthing

As already mentioned, the lock gates open $2\frac{1}{2}$ hours before local HW and close $3\frac{1}{2}$ hours after except at neaps, when the period can be shortened by up to 15 minutes at each end. In the event of arrival too early, the best water will be found close in along the north side of the outer breakwater, and unless there is an onshore swell it is usually possible to secure alongside a fishing boat until the gates open, although of course the boat should not be left unmanned in such a position.

Once the gates open, traffic-type signals are used to control passage, and must be closely observed, as visibility of oncoming traffic is very bad from either side. A green light permits passage, a red one forbids it: note that this differs from most signal systems further west where green permits entry and red permits exit, the same light being displayed in both directions.

61. St Vaast in the old days when yachts dried out alongside on the stinking mud.

62. St Vaast-la-Hougue: view of Ile Tatihou from St Vaast.

Having entered the basin, berth on the pontoons as directed or as space allows: no fewer than 130 berths are at present reserved for yachts on passage.

Water on the pontoons; fuel from pumps below the Capitainerie, immediately on the starboard hand after entry: this building also houses showers, toilets and clubhouse. (I use the present tense, but these are in fact plans for the 1983 season.) The charming town provides excellent shops and restaurants: there is a chandler, St Vaast Plaisance, on the Quai Vauban overlooking the harbour, a boatyard, Chantiers Bernard, capable of repairs, and M. Pierre Conraud, who has a garage at 12 rue des Salinas (Tel. (33) 54-41-54) is a Perkins agent and is experienced in repairing marine engines of all makes.

Tidal information
Range at Mean springs: 5·2 metres; Mean neaps: 3·2 metres.
The north-going stream starts at HW Dover $-\frac{1}{2}$; the south-going stream at HW Dover $+5\frac{1}{2}$.
Rates in the St Vaast area do not normally much exceed one knot.

Barfleur

Charts Nos. 1106 and 2073

This is a charming harbour, with a beautiful church, first-class hotels and attractive architecture. Some nine hundred years ago William the Conquerer knew it well.

Unfortunately the harbour dries and it is quite unprotected from winds between N and E, with the result that with very strong NE winds the scend in the harbour causes some heavy bumping when boats take or leave the ground. If caught in such conditions, consult the harbourmaster, who may be able to allot a mooring buoy where the boat will dry onto soft mud.

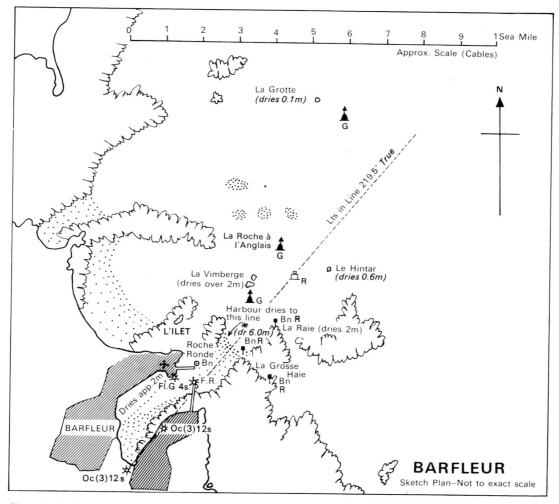

Plan 26   Barfleur.

63. Barfleur: the entrance from La Roche à l'Anglais buoy.

Tidal streams outside the harbour are not strong and run at not more than 2 knots, to the N about −05·00 hours before HW Dover and to the S about +00·30 hours after HW Dover. Between three and one hour before local HW is the best time to enter the harbour, but it is not advisable in very strong onshore winds. HW Barfleur is 2·14 hours before HW Dover and 55 minutes after Cherbourg at mean tides.

Approach and Entrance
From seaward, a valuable landmark is the immensely tall tower of the lighthouse on Cap Barfleur, which also transmits a radio beacon, F G (·· —· — —·) on 291·9 kHz. Care must be taken to avoid passing through the Barfleur Race in anything but calm weather, particularly with wind over tide. For further details on this, see Passage Notes Barfleur to Cherbourg on page 112.

The entrance looks alarming on the Admiralty Chart, but this is largely because of the confusion which a high degree of detail can produce. In fact it is very well marked, and perfectly simple to follow.

64. Barfleur: *Le Hintar*, first port hand mark.

From either direction, keep at least 1½ miles offshore until northeast of the town, which is easily recognisable by its church, which looks from seaward rather like a castle. Approaching from this direction, steer straight for the church, adjusting the course for tidal set to remain on a SW (mag.) course for the town. When just under a mile from the pierheads, a green buoy, La Grotte, will be seen to starboard. This should be left about 1½ cables to starboard, when a pair of green and red buoys will be seen ahead . Pass between these (the red one is Le Hintar), and then steer for the first of two port hand beacons with cylinder topmarks. Pass both of these close on their starboard side, and then steer straight for the entrance. A third port hand beacon between and to the south of the two referred to should be ignored. At night there is no problem, as the leading lights, Oc (3) 12s, lead straight through all the hazards. Follow the line until close in to the south pierhead, Oc R 4s, then steer to north of it and into the harbour. Entry at night is really easier than in daylight, as is often the case in the similar North Breton harbours. Of course, if a course on the leading lights were maintained too long, a collision with

65. Barfleur: the next port hand mark (beacon).

the outside of the south breakwater would result, but in fact the lights disappear behind the wall before this danger develops.

For shelter from westerly winds, it is possible to enter to just inside the pierheads as much as four hours before or after high water: at that time there is 1·5 metres of water at a top spring, and 2·2 metres at neaps. One can anchor there and wait for enough water to go alongside.

Berthing

Yachts should berth along the south-west half of the NW wall of the harbour. There are small ladders all along the wall, and the bottom is firm sand and fairly flat. The SW wall is mostly used by fishermen, and the SE side is shoal and foul. A friendly harbourmaster (Tel. (33) 54-02-68) will advise (and collect dues). Good shops and restaurants, and a charming town.

66. Barfleur: the last port hand mark (beacon).

67. Barfleur: the harbour at high water . . .

68. . . . and low water. Note extent of drying rock by beacon outside entrance.

Tidal information

HEIGHT ABOVE DATUM OF SOUNDINGS IN METRES

High water		*Low water*	
Mean springs	Mean neaps	Mean springs	Mean neaps
6·4	5·1	0·9	2·3

The north-going stream starts at HW Dover $-\frac{1}{2}$, the south-going stream at HW Dover $+5\frac{1}{2}$.

Plan 27 Barfleur Lighthouse.

Races arise when the tide is accelerated by a headland or promontory, and they are intensified when the fast stream thus created has to pass over a rough bottom. The Barfleur Race has both these characteristics in generous measure, and it is often a thoroughly unpleasant and dangerous piece of water. In a heavy NW blow, the seas on the ebb are ferocious, and could easily overwhelm a yacht, and in such conditions the point of the Cape should be given an offing of at least seven miles, and even then the effects of the race will be clearly felt. In these conditions the ebb outside Barfleur will tend to draw one up into the danger, so it is important to leave before high water to get a good offing before this effect develops. A similar offing is needed in a SE wind on the flood. The distance off from Barfleur Light can be found in seconds with a sextant—even a cheap plastic one—and the tables in Reeds. If by misfortune you find yourself in the race, keep the engine running, as the strong eddies and whirlpools can twist a sailing vessel round, gybing her or heaving her to unexpectedly, thus making sailing almost impossible. In calm weather it is safe to pass through the race, but the sea can get up in minutes if even a moderate breeze develops. In any strong wind it is safest to pass through the race at slack water (HW Dover -1 or $+5$).

Tide-rips may be met at other places between Cherbourg and Barfleur, notably off Cap Lévi where severe seas can be encountered in wind-over-tide conditions, especially when the E-going stream meets a strong NE wind.

Plan 28   Cap Lévi Lighthouse.

Both of these are very small fishing harbours and there is little object in staying in either, although they are both worth a visit at high water for those who like to explore every nook and cranny of the French coast. Both are drying harbours open to winds SW through W to N in the case of Port de Lévi and NW to NE in the case of Port du Becquet.

Port de Lévi

There are no leading lights, but the light structure is sectored and gives fixed red, green, and white, and it is extremely important to stay in the green sector to avoid the outlying hazards. You are strongly advised not to make this entrance at night because there are numerous lobster pots and their cork floats are impossible to see.

In daytime the white marks on each side of the harbour are clearly visible and entrance should be effected when the white structure on the wall (on which the light is mounted) is midway between them.

69. Port de Lévi: entrance to the harbour.

70. Port de Lévi: mooring should be alongside the wall at right. Note Cap Lévi lighthouse in the background on the extreme right.

When inside the harbour avoid the southern side, but make fast to the wall on the NE side, below the white building.

The tidal stream outside the harbour is no stronger than at Port du Becquet but it behaves differently, as follows: it sets to the N +1·00 hour to −3·00 hours and to the S −3·00 hours to +1 hour on Dover.

Port de Lévi has no village of its own, but Fermanville is only fifteen minutes' walk and has the essentials for shopping plus a small restaurant; its proprietor is an important man in the place and is full of information.

The lighthouse at Cap Lévi is a stone structure, built in 1947. The previous one was destroyed in the last war. The light is a very powerful one, Fl R 5s, visible 22 miles.

Port du Becquet

There are leading lights for this place; that situated further inland gives Oc (3) R 12s. The nearer one, Oc (3) W 12s, is synchronised with the red one. The latter has an intense sector. The two lights are in line on 187° True. They are clear to see when making Cherbourg harbour, particularly when swept by the tide too far to the eastward. By day the two white towers housing these lights are visible: as is a red beacon tower surmounted by a red cylinder just to the east of the entrance, named La Tournette.

There is only one possible place to lie and this is the southern side of the jetty which runs E and W. The tidal streams outside the harbour should be given consideration; these are as follows:

The tide begins running to the E +0·40 and to the W −05·50 on Dover (maximum speed 2 knots).

There is considerable scend with any onshore swell.

71. Port du Becquet: note beacon on left of picture, leading lights on the right.

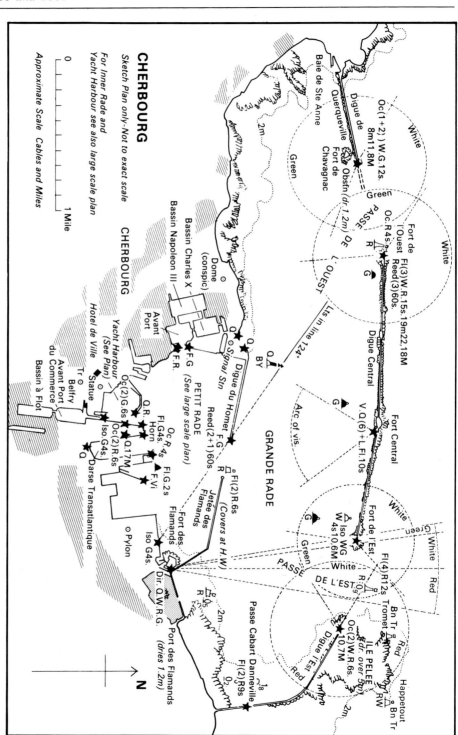

CHERBOURG

Sketch Plan only-Not to exact scale

For Inner Rade and Yacht Harbour see also large scale plan

Approximate Scale Cables and Miles

0   1 Mile

Plan 29   Cherbourg: an overall plan.

116

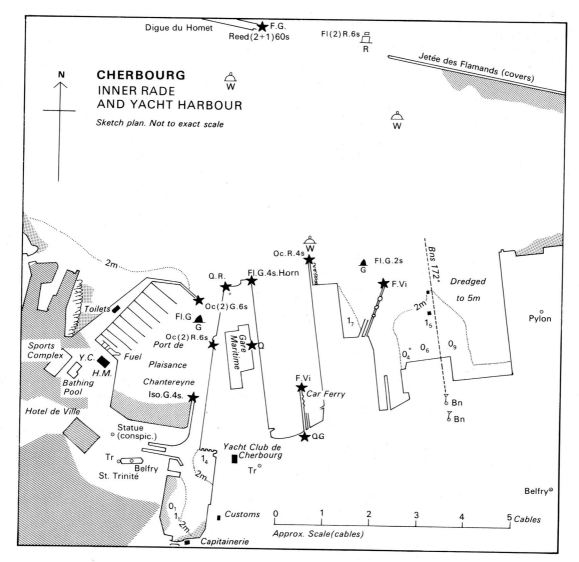

Digee du Homet   F.G.
Reed(2+1)60s   Fl(2)R.6s
    R

Jetée des Flamands (covers)

CHERBOURG
INNER RADE
AND YACHT HARBOUR
W

Sketch plan. Not to exact scale

N

W

Oc.R.4s
W
Fl.G.2s
G

Bns 172°

Dredged
to 5m

F.Vi

Q.R.
Fl.G.4s.Horn

Oc(2)G.6s

2m

2m

Toilets

Fl.G
G

Oc(2)R.6s

Port de

Plaisance

Gare
Maritime

Q

1₇

2m
1₅

0₄
0₆
0₉

Pylon

Sports
Complex
Y.C.
H.M.

Fuel

Chantereyne

Iso.G.4s.

F.Vi

Car Ferry

Bn

Bn

Bathing
Pool

Hotel de Ville

Statue
(conspic.)

Tr
Belfry
St. Trinité

1₄

2m

Yacht Club de
Cherbourg

Tr

Belfry

Q.G

0₁
1₄
2m

Customs

Capitainerie

Approx. Scale(cables)

0   1   2   3   4   5 *Cables*

Plan 30   Cherbourg: Inner Rade and yacht harbour.

Cherbourg is arguably the most important yachting port on the whole of the north coast of France, providing as it does a yacht harbour with over 700 berths (1982), available at all states of the tide and in all weathers, and offering every possible facility for repair and service. It is also pleasant to record that its charges, at least as late as 1982, were extremely modest in comparison with other harbours covered in this book, certainly taking into account the excellence of the facilities.

As well as being a yachting port, Cherbourg is of course also a commercial and fishing port, an important naval base and, geographically, for yachtsmen, it is the gateway to the Channel Islands and the coast of Brittany.

The distance between Cherbourg and the Nab is roughly 60 sea miles. An inexperienced yachtsman may be tempted to call this a twelve-hour passage, so that the tidal streams on the French coast will equal the tidal streams on the English coast, but nothing could be more misleading, as many people have discovered; it is vital that the course with tidal corrections should be plotted regularly. One reason why this is so important is because there is *always* some haze over Cherbourg and it is a very difficult place to identify from a distance of, say, 15 miles. By the time the breakwater is positively identified, at perhaps a distance of nine miles, the tide, which may be running at more than four knots, has taken the yacht in the direction of Cap de la Hague, or—worse still—into the difficult waters E of Cherbourg.

In bad visibility it is possible to obtain a good position by taking bearings of radio beacons and at night by taking bearings of the lights of Cap de la Hague and Barfleur. Fort de l'Ouest radiobeacon (RB · — · — ···) transmits on 312·6 kHz every 2 minutes (range 20 miles).

Cherbourg has three entrances, the Passe Cabart Danneville, at the SE corner of the great mole (which encloses the outer or main harbour), the eastern entrance, and the western entrance. No-one would automatically or accidentally pick the first of these and indeed there is rather a strong tidal stream at this position—it is therefore usually a choice of the eastern or the western entrance.

Approach

The approach from the east has been covered to some extent under the notes on the Barfleur Race. It is possible for experienced yachtsmen with local knowledge to pass inside the three

72. Cherbourg: the eastern entrance (and opposite).

118

buoys that mark the hazards north and west of Cap Barfleur (Les Equets, Basses du Rénier and La Pierre Noire), but this should only be attempted in good weather and visibility and after the landmarks are known. A passage outside these buoys is safe and straightforward.

The approach from the west, once the Cherbourg peninsular is well abeam, presents no particular difficulties. It should however be mentioned that the tidal streams flow strongly right across the north of the peninsular, and many yachts have been swept into the Barfleur Race to the east or the Alderney Race to the west, usually by trying to sail when there is not enough wind. This tidal factor is of the greatest importance on the approach from the north, and it is vital to continue to steer a course which allows for the tide right up to the entrance chosen, and resist the temptation to steer for the heads once they are sighted, as that inevitably results in being swept down-tide of them: an error from which it often takes hours to recover.

The choice of which of the two main entrances to use depends on the direction of approach, or on the landfall if coming from the north. The Passe Cabart Danneville is only useful when approaching from the east and cheating a foul tide: it should only be used at at least half tide, when there is at least 1·7 m over the nearby shoals: stream through the passe can reach 5 knots at springs.

There is no problem with using the western entrance, the only hazard being an unmarked extension, awash at an average low water, which projects about 150 metres beyond the end of the Digue de Querqueville, the most westerly of the three outer breakwaters. Care must be taken with the eastern entrance, however, particularly at night. The rocks of the Ile Pelée

73. Cherbourg: the eastern entrance (and opposite).

extend nearly $\frac{1}{2}$ mile north of the breakwater, and are marked only by two unlit beacon towers: Happetout to the east, and Tromet to the west. Coming from the east at night, it is therefore important to give the Ile Pelée light a good berth until the light on the Fort de l'Est changes from green to white (Iso. 4 secs.). It is then safe to steer for the Fort de l'Est, keeping in the white sector, until Ile Pelee light turns white, then turn SE into the Grande Rade. Chart 2602 will make clear what I mean.

Entrance and Berthing
Once inside the Grande Rade, the first thing to do is to identify the entrance to the Petite Rade, or inner harbour. This lies ESE from the western entrance, or SW from the eastern one, and is marked by a F.G. light on the end of the Digue du Homet to starboard, and a red buoy, Fl (2) R 6s, to port. The latter is just clear of the end of the Jetée des Flamands, part of which covers at high tide. Pass midway between these two marks, and from here a course of 205° (mag.) leads into the yacht harbour. This lies immediately to the west of the main ferry and liner port, which is brightly lit, and indeed the plethora of lights, both navigational and shore, can be confusing until one is used to it. However just to starboard of the brightest shore lights, it should be possible to pick out the lights marking the entrance to the yacht harbour, QR to port and Oc (2) G6s to starboard. Once in, the yacht harbour is well lit at night. Berth on a pontoon as space allows: in working hours an official may indicate a free berth.

Facilities
As has already been said, the facilities offered at Cherbourg are now outstanding, and it was a pleasant surprise in 1982 to find that the dues were no more than average, thus representing

74. Cherbourg: entrance to the yacht harbour from the Petite Rade.

outstanding value for money. Water and electricity are available on all pontoons, and there is a fuelling pier. In 1982 this was available three hours either side of HW, but only between 0800 and 1400 or 1500 to 2000; ultimately it is hoped to dredge it so that it can be used at any time. It is a structure of iron girders, and risky to moor to if the wind is blowing onto it. There are showers and toilets at the Capitainerie, and an additional lot on the main west pier open 0900-1145 and 1400-1730, with a small annexe open 24 hours a day. The large and comfortable yacht club (Tel. (33) 53-02-83) has a bar where sandwiches are available, and its own showers. The bar is closed on Wednesdays. This is now the headquarters of the Yacht Club de Cherbourg, who have moved there from their old building overlooking the Avant-Port.

75. Cherbourg: the yacht harbour. The yacht club is on the left, with the fuelling jetty.

The Capitainerie (Tel. 53-75-16: also listens out on Channel 9) is always manned and endlessly helpful: it is in the large building near the root of the main pier which also houses the club. Cherbourg Marine (Tel. 43-11-36), which are opposite the club building, undertake all kinds of repairs, and are excellent chandlers. They have no sailmaker, but will put visitors in touch with one in the town. The town, which has great character, and lies only a few hundred metres south of the yacht harbour, offers all possible facilities in the way of shopping, restaurants etc. Duty free stores are available beside the club: French charts at Nicollet, 140 Rue du Commerce, or from the Cherbourg General Yachting, at the rear of the duty-free shop just W of the club.

Omonville-la-Rogue

Charts Nos. 1106 and 2669

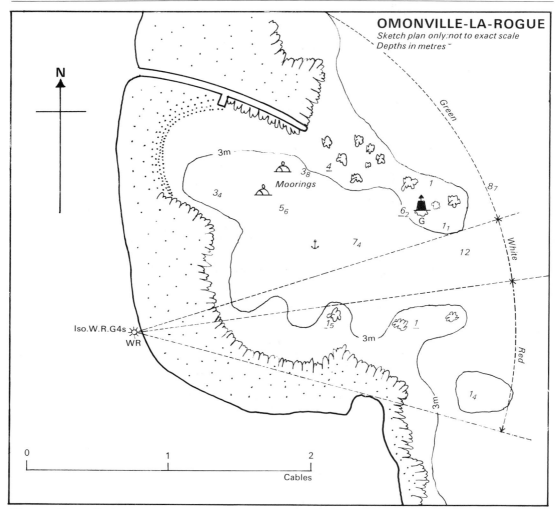

OMONVILLE-LA-ROGUE
*Sketch plan only:not to exact scale
Depths in metres*

N

3m
3₈
4
Moorings
3₄
5₆
1
8₇
6₂
G
1₁
⌖
7₄
12
White
Iso.W.R.G4s
WR
1₅
1
3m
Red
3m
1₄

0   1   2
Cables

Plan 31   Omonville-la-Rogue.

This small harbour lies some seven miles west of Cherbourg's western entrance, and provides good protection from all but winds from the eastern sector. The approach is straightforward by day, the entrance lying a cable S of Le Tunard beacon, and at night the white sector of the harbour light leads in clear of all hazards. There are two large visitors' buoys: several yachts can moor to each buoy, each using their own stern anchor. There is a restaurant and one or two shops in the village, which is about half a mile from the harbour. This is a useful place to spend a night after passing through the Alderney Race on the last of the N. E-going tide, and it is a pretty enough place in its own right.

122

Passage Notes: Cherbourg to Channel Islands and West Cotentin

Apart from the few who intend merely to visit Omonville and return, most people who sail westwards from Cherbourg along the north Cotentin coast intend to visit the Channel Islands or, less probably, the west coast ports of Cotentin. In either case, the Alderney Race has to be reckoned with, and this is potentially one of the most dangerous stretches of water in Europe, and should always be treated with great respect.

Having said this, let me make it clear at once that there is no problem in navigating this area, as long as careful attention is paid to timing. If wind is with tide (and of course both must then be favourable, or no progress will be made) the overfalls and eddies that occur in the race are not dangerous, and indeed nothing could be greater fun than sailing through the race at the height of the stream with a moderate following breeze, perhaps attaining ten knots over the ground. Even in such conditions, however, strong swirls may be encountered, and unexpected gybes are always a risk that the whole crew should be prepared for.

The problems arise in wind-over-tide conditions (or in really strong winds from any direction, when the whole area is really best avoided). It is difficult to lay down definite wind forces where the conditions become unacceptably bad, but certainly passing through the Race with the full force of a mean tide against a SW wind force 4 produced some very steep seas when I tried it recently, and I would not have cared for the experience had there been an extra force in the wind, or had it been a day or two nearer spring tides. That was motoring into the wind: sailing is made more difficult by the sudden patches of steep seas and swirls of tide: I remember on one occasion being put right about under sail and finding myself hove to.

Going Southwest through the Race, the prudent thing to do is to arrive north of Cap de la Hague just as the fair tide is beginning, thus getting through the worst area long before the stream, and therefore the overfalls, has reached its peak. This is facilitated by the fact that there is a westgoing eddy running inshore along most of the coast from Cherbourg to Cap de la Hague during most of the eastgoing stream. An average yacht leaving Cherbourg three hours before HW Dover should therefore reach the Cap at or a little before HW Dover, when the stream is slack in the east part of the race, and just beginning to run SW on the Alderney side. With this timing the worst area of overfalls will be far behind by the time the stream reaches its maximum rate three hours after HW Dover. Be warned, however, that patches of tide-race conditions can be met under such circumstances almost anywhere between Cap de la Hague and Guernsey, especially near springs, and in any but good conditions care should be taken to avoid passing over the Alderney South Banks or the Banc de la Schole, which can both produce bad seas.

On the NE-going tide, the overfalls occur mostly at the NE end of the race, beyond Alderney, and here the aim must be to pass through the race well over towards the Alderney side, passing about three miles east of the SW corner of Alderney $2\frac{1}{2}$ to 2 hours before HW Dover. The boat will then pass through the worst part of the race on the last of the tide, and can buck the foul tide to Cherbourg or wait for a fair one at Omonville according to circumstances.

The passage to Alderney itself avoids the main part of the race, but great care must be taken not to be swept unwillingly into it, especially near springs. Notes on the Swinge, the channel north of Alderney, will be found in the section on that island.

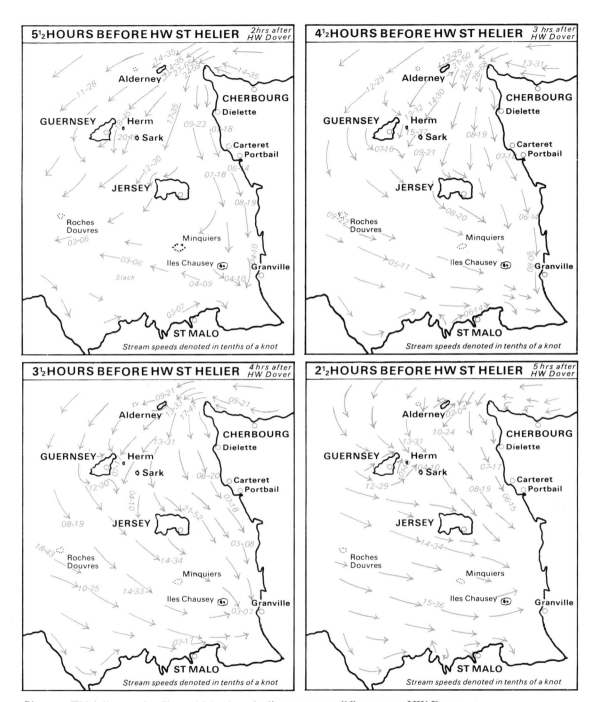

Plan 32   Tidal diagram for Channel Islands and adjacent coasts: differences on HW Dover.

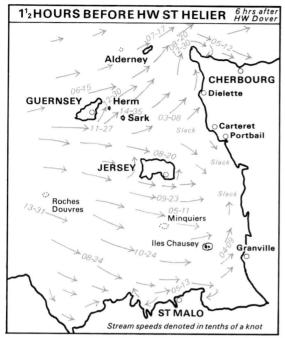

1½ HOURS BEFORE HW ST HELIER *6 hrs after HW Dover*

Alderney
CHERBOURG
Dielette
GUERNSEY
Herm
Sark
Carteret
Portbail
Slack
JERSEY
Slack
Roches
Douvres
Minquiers
Slack
Iles Chausey
Granville
ST MALO

Stream speeds denoted in tenths of a knot

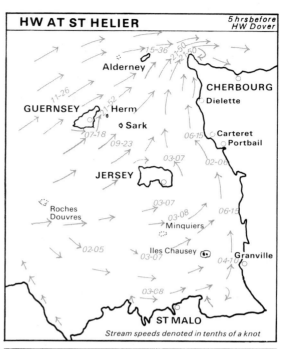

HW AT ST HELIER *5 hrs before HW Dover*

Alderney
CHERBOURG
Dielette
GUERNSEY
Herm
Sark
Carteret
Portbail
JERSEY
Roches
Douvres
Minquiers
Iles Chausey
Granville
ST MALO

Stream speeds denoted in tenths of a knot

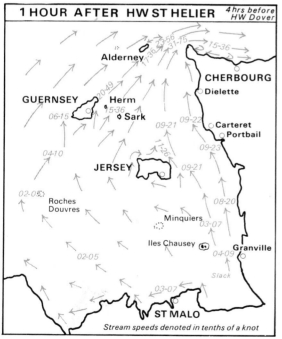

1 HOUR AFTER HW ST HELIER *4 hrs before HW Dover*

Alderney
CHERBOURG
Dielette
GUERNSEY
Herm
Sark
Carteret
Portbail
JERSEY
Roches
Douvres
Minquiers
Iles Chausey
Granville
Slack
ST MALO

Stream speeds denoted in tenths of a knot

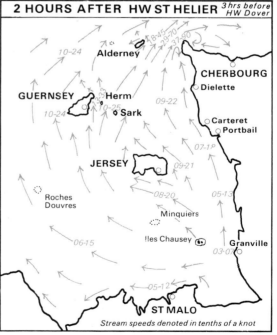

2 HOURS AFTER HW ST HELIER *3 hrs before HW Dover*

Alderney
CHERBOURG
Dielette
GUERNSEY
Herm
Sark
Carteret
Portbail
JERSEY
Roches
Douvres
Minquiers
Iles Chausey
Granville
ST MALO

Stream speeds denoted in tenths of a knot

125

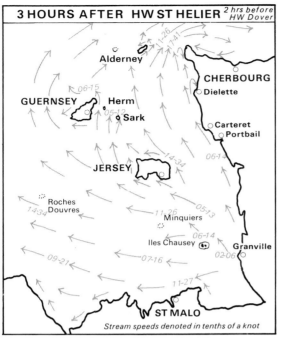

3 HOURS AFTER HW ST HELIER *2 hrs before HW Dover*

Alderney

CHERBOURG
○ Dielette

GUERNSEY Herm
○ Sark
06-15

05-12

○ Carteret
○ Portbail

JERSEY

14-34
06-14

Roches
Douvres
14-34

11-26
Minquiers

05-13

06-14
Iles Chausey ⦿
02-06
○ Granville

09-21
07-16

11-27

ST MALO
Stream speeds denoted in tenths of a knot

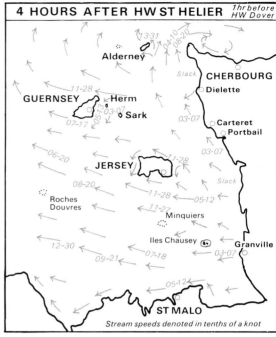

4 HOURS AFTER HW ST HELIER *1 hr before HW Dover*

Alderney

Slack
CHERBOURG
○ Dielette

GUERNSEY *11-28* Herm
○ Sark
07-17 *05-13* *03-07*

03-07
○ Carteret
○ Portbail

06-20

JERSEY *11-28*

08-20

Slack

11-28 *05-12*
11-27

Roches
Douvres

Minquiers

12-30
Iles Chausey ⦿
Granville

09-21 *07-18* *03-07*

05-12

ST MALO
Stream speeds denoted in tenths of a knot

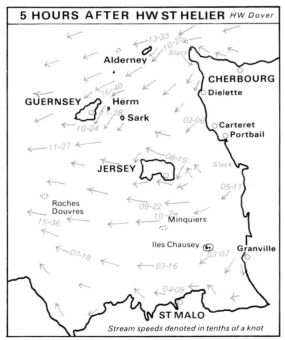

5 HOURS AFTER HW ST HELIER *HW Dover*

13-33
10-25
Alderney
Slack

CHERBOURG
○ Dielette

16-40

GUERNSEY Herm
11-28 ○ Sark
10-24

02-06
○ Carteret
○ Portbail

11-27

08-19
JERSEY
Slack

Roches
Douvres
15-36

09-22

05-11

10-24
Minquiers

Iles Chausey ⦿
03-07
Granville

07-18
07-16

04-09

ST MALO
Stream speeds denoted in tenths of a knot

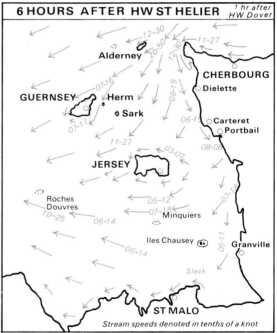

6 HOURS AFTER HW ST HELIER *1 hr after HW Dover*

12-30
10-50
Alderney *11-27*
12-30

CHERBOURG
○ Dielette

07-16
08-19

GUERNSEY Herm
○ Sark
07-17
06-15
○ Carteret
○ Portbail

11-27

08-08
JERSEY
03-07

Roches
Douvres
10-25

05-12
07-18
07-19
Minquiers

06-14

06-14
Iles Chausey ⦿
05-11
Granville

Slack

ST MALO
Stream speeds denoted in tenths of a knot

126

The Ports of West Cotentin

Goury

Chart No. 1106, French 5636

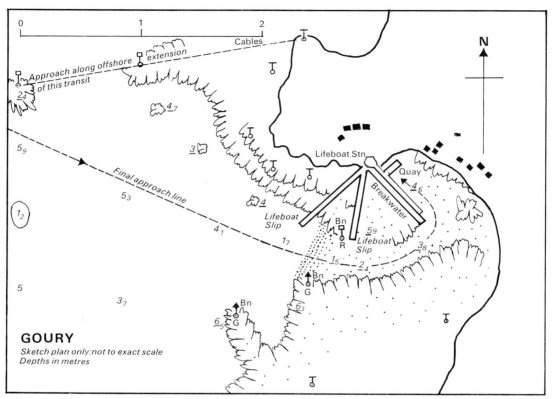

Plan 33   Goury.

Little more than half a mile SSW of Cap de la Hague light, and approached from the Alderney Race, this is not a harbour for the inexperienced, and it is more a place of interest to the dedicated explorer than one that has much practical value on passage.

Approach

La Fordine YBY beacon tower must first be located, about a mile WSW of the Cap de la Hague lighthouse. Coming from the north, the tower must not be approached from any direction east of north: from the south keep a mile offshore until it is reached. From a position 100 m S of the beacon, two red beacons will be seen bearing almost exactly magnetic east. If these are kept in line, this leads close but safely south of the dangerous La Magne rock (dr. 4 m). When 200 m short of the front beacon, turn SE for the harbour, leaving G beacons to starboard and R to port.

76. Goury: the two beacons on the right of picture are left to starboard, and with a little more rise of tide one can enter past the pierhead.

Berthing

There is some 3 m inside the jetty at HW Neaps, and about $4\frac{1}{2}$ m at HWS. The problem is that the Race is slack off Goury at HW and HW $+5\frac{1}{2}$ Dover. At HW Dover it is still $2\frac{1}{2}$ hours before HW Goury, and it may well be necessary to anchor off the entrance for an hour before there is enough water to enter and berth as space and local advice permit. The other slack is really useless, as this comes about three hours after HW Goury, and it would be necessary to wait for seven hours or so before entering. However, by using the inshore eddy, it is possible to time arrival either from Cherbourg or from the south at the HW Dover slack. French chart 5636 should be carried on any visit to Goury.

The Passage inside the Gros du Raz

77. On line for the passage inside the Gros du Raz, a tricky and dangerous short cut which is *not* recommended.

The main lighthouse that marks Cap de la Hague stands in fact on an offshore islet called the Gros du Raz, and it is possible to sail between the lighthouse and the mainland. This provides a short cut on the passage from Goury to Cherbourg. It is, however, an extremely tricky piece of navigation past unmarked rocks, and I do not recommend anyone to attempt it. If it is to be tried, it should only be under ideal conditions near the HW Dover slack, when at a suitable tide La Plate rock (dr. 5·4 m) should be just visible. Passing half-way between the Gros and La Plate from a position one cable W of the outer of the leading beacons for Goury, continue on about 15° True until the N Cardinal beacon N of the lighthouse is abeam, then N True for two cables, after which it is safe to steer NW for the open sea. A close watch must be kept at all times for tidal effects, which must be counteracted, and French chart 5636 is vital. According to my observations, the tide turns N in this channel about an hour before it changes in the main race offshore. I must emphasize that this is a difficult and potentially dangerous passage, and any reader attempting it does so at his own risk.

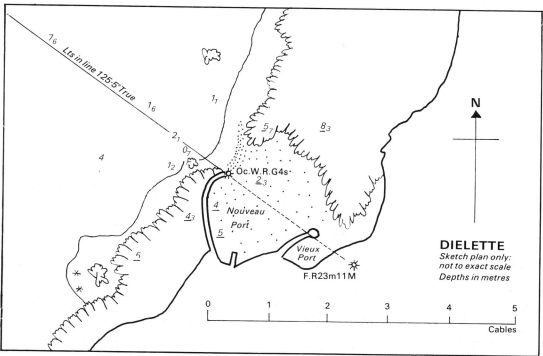

Plan 34 Dielette.

This small fishing harbour dries completely at LW, and unfortunately the whole of the sheltered area behind the breakwater is criss-crossed by mooring lines, some sunken and some floating, used by the local fishermen. Approach on the line of the two lighthouses at night: in daylight the rear lighthouse is hard to identify, as it is housed in an ordinary house (high, with a steeply pitched roof) but the white patch on the old (inner) pierhead just open of the one on the end of the new (outer) breakwater makes a safe line. Keep close to the breakwater head entering to avoid the mass of drying rocks which act as a natural breakwater, and extend to within 100 m of the breakwater head from the northern arm of the bay.

In calm or offshore weather there is no problem over berthing: anchor clear of the moorings. This position is poorly sheltered, however, and is not safe in onshore winds as severe pounding will be suffered when drying. I have spent a comfortable night alongside a fisherman just inside the breakwater head, but at the cost of a (fortunately incomprehensible, owing to the thick Norman accent) dressing down from another fisherman who considered I was in his way. It is also possible to anchor in the inner Vieux Port in rather better shelter and take a stern line ashore, but this is shallow and probably has only a couple of feet of water at HW neaps, although up to three metres at HWS.

There is a butcher in the village, but no other shops. There is also a hotel (the menus looked very expensive to me) and a small bar-restaurant.

78. Dielette: *Kuri Moana* is moored (and aground) just inside the breakwater head. The drying reefs referred to in the text can be clearly seen: unfortunately they provide little shelter near high water.

Carteret

Chart No. 2669

This pleasant little town is mainly a holiday resort, but there is still a considerable fishing fleet. There is space for a few visiting yachts, either drying on moorings, or against a quay or a fishing boat.

Approach and Entry

The entrance lies about ½ mile east of the large Cap de Carteret light (Fl (2 + 1) 15s 81 m 26 M) and there is an Oc R 4s light on the head of the main west jetty, which is left close to port when entering. Tides are almost identical in height and timing with St Helier. The outer part of the

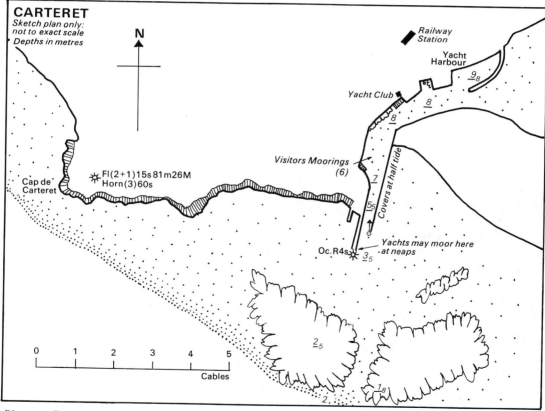

Plan 35   Carteret.

entrance channel dries only 3–4 metres, so with a half-tide level of over 6 metres it is possible to reach the shelter of the west jetty at any time after half tide, but to enter the inner part of the harbour, which dries 7–9 metres, it is necessary to wait until near high water, and even then the upper parts remain dry at neaps. The approach is straighforward in daylight: keeping the east side of the jetty just open gives a good approach line, and warns if the boat is being swept off line by the stream.

Berthing and Facilities

The ferry to Gorey berths along the inner half of the west jetty (the eastern one is a breakwater covering at half-tide, whose end is marked by a green beacon), but yachts are permitted to berth alongside the outer part at neap tides only. Otherwise proceed inwards past the fish quay and the slip: there is a small amount of wall beyond here that is reserved for yachts, and six visitors' moorings (which, of course, dry) each with a separate bow and stern warp. Further up still, beyond a small basin which should not be used without local advice, as the bottom is foul, is a small yacht basin which few visiting boats would be able to reach except at high springs, as it dries 9·8 metres, and so has 1–1½ metres at HW on a good spring. However, it is often possible to

79. Carteret looms out of the mist. The beacon just left of the motor boat marks the end of the covering east jetty.

134

moor alongside a fisherman for a couple of tides in the lower part of the harbour if the visitors' area is full, by finding one who is not intending to go out, or who is already aground on a falling tide. This is a pretty little town with excellent shops conveniently close to the harbour.

80. Carteret. It is often possible to moor on the fishing quay if a boat can be found that is not intending to go out.

Portbail

Chart No. 2669

This is an interesting little harbour, and beyond the harbour itself lies a huge expanse of drying sand where it is possible to dry out at anchor with suitable precautions (and not in strong SW winds).

Approach and Entry

The tall elegant white water tower just north of the entrance is a valuable landmark, as there is little else to see until close in. There are extensive offshore shoals, but these will be well covered long before it is safe to approach the harbour, which according to observations I made in 1982 dries almost exactly 5 m along the best approach line. It is best to approach just after high water to avoid being swept in too fast by the flood, but be warned that the ebb can exceed five knots at springs, so do not be late.

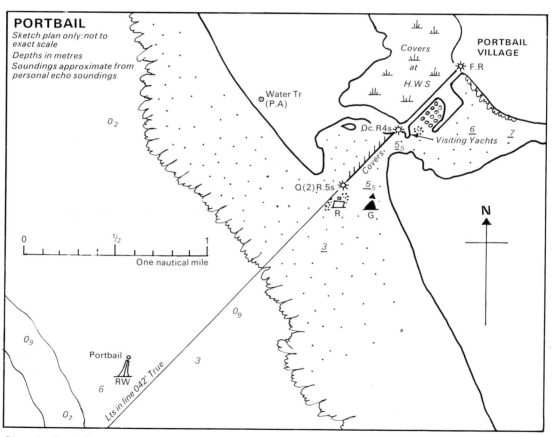

Plan 36 Portbail.

From the RW offing buoy make for the R beacon marking the end of the training wall after passing midway between the two entrance buoys. Leave the beacon to port about 5 metres off and proceed along the training wall (it submerges, but is marked by pole beacons) until abreast of the second-last pole. From here steer straight for the jetty head until 50 m off, then alter course slightly to starboard so as to leave the end of the jetty 10 metres to port, then turn sharp to port and enter the basin close along the east side of the jetty. The outer (wood-faced) part of the jetty is the ferry berth, and has a ledge projecting a metre outwards under water.

Berthing and Facilities

The inner part of the jetty's E side is reserved for fishermen and yachts, their allocations being clearly painted on the wall. Moor alongside the yacht part of the wall, or another yacht. There are also numerous moorings in the basin, and one of these can be picked up if free, although of

81. Portbail: the entrance from the head of the jetty. Steering for here from the second last beacon pole gives the best water.

course the boat should not be left uncrewed until it is clear that the owner cannot return on the tide in question. If going to the moorings, the best line is to cut diagonally from the jetty head to the inside of the mole and then along the moorings: a bank builds up between the deep water near the jetty and the fairly deep water where the moorings are. (Deep is of course comparative: the whole harbour dries). The jetty moorings can be reached 1½ hours either side of HW at neaps, the buoys one hour either side, by a boat with 1·5 m draft. These times extend by half an hour at each end at springs.

There is a bar 100 metres to seaward of the jetty, which is open seven days a week and provides light meals (grills) and ices etc. as well as drinks. All other supplies from the charming town, about half a mile to the NE across the causeway. There are two interesting churches, and some fine old buildings. A pleasant and interesting place well worth a visit.

82. Portbail. The yacht space in the harbour is not very extensive, but at least it is clearly marked.

Granville

Chart No. 2669

Now an important yacht harbour, Granville boasts of having the largest tidal range of any port in Europe, and indeed the 12 m spring range means that at the height of the flood the tide can rise by 3 m in an hour, or five centimetres in a minute! In spite of these impressive figures the harbour presents no particular problems.

Approach and Entry

The sill which protects the yacht basin dries 6 m, but there is a gap in the sill drying only 5·25 m, closed by a gate 0·75 m high, thus bringing the height in line with the rest of the sill. When the water rises above the sill the gate begins to fall, and by the time there is 65 cm of water over the sill the gate is fully open and there is 1·4 m available over the gate. An illuminated display on the S breakwater shows the depth over the gate: this goes straight from 0 to 1·3 on a rising tide, and

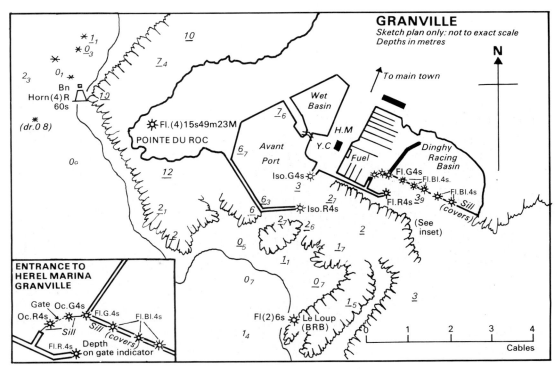

Plan 37   Granville.

139

from 1·3 to 0 on a falling one: it is strictly prohibited to attempt to cross the gate even a moment after the display has changed to zero. The gate lies between a red and a green column: Oc R 4s and Oc G 4s respectively.

The approach is straightforward, with no hazards offshore at a tide level where there will be water over the sill. The Pointe du Roc, just W of the entrance, is craggy and unmistakeable, with a lighthouse (Fl (4) 15s) visible 22 miles: pass ½ mile south of this, leave Le Loup BRB beacon tower (Fl (2) 6s), to port and steer for the entrance, which is round the E end of the more easterly of the two visible east-pointing pierheads. Do not enter unless there is enough water shown on the indicator to enable the boat to be taken straight over the gate between the two columns, and into the yacht harbour. The Avant port to the west can be used to wait in shelter for sufficient rise of tide: there is a repeater depth indicator there. The bottom is hard mud and reasonably clear, so it would be possible to dry out there in an emergency if too late for the gate.

83. Granville with the Pointe du Roc lighthouse to the left, from Le Loup.

84. Granville yacht harbour at low water, showing the sill and gate.

Berthing and Facilities

The berths are normal marina berths: 150 are reserved for visitors. Fuel is available from a fuel berth: open 8–12 and 2–6: for service apply to the marina office. There are showers and 24 hour toilets, which were unisex in 1982. There are numerous chandlers capable of all repairs, and a sailmaker. Good shops in the town, about 300 metres. I did not find the town itself to be of great interest, but the marina is a pleasant place. Useful names and numbers include:

Marina office (Capitaine M. D. Denis) Tel: (33) 50-20-06

Y.C. de Granville, quai Ouest, Tel: 50-04-25 (Clubhouse, with showers etc.)

Customs, rue du Port, Tel: 50-19-90

Weather reports (recorded), Tel: 50-10-00

Rothéneuf

Charts Nos. 2700, 3659, 2669

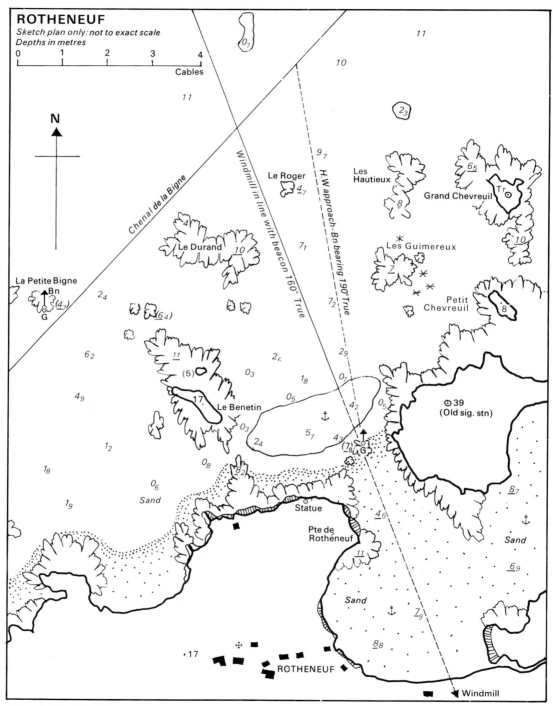

ROTHENEUF

Sketch plan only: not to exact scale
Depths in metres

0 1 2 3 4
Cables

N

Chenal de la Bigne

Windmill in line with beacon 160° True

H.W approach - Bn bearing 190° True

0_7

11

10

11

2_3

9_7

Les
Hautieux

8

Le Roger
4_7

6_5

Grand Chevreuil
Tr

10

7_1

Les Guimereux
7

7_2

2_9

Petit
Chevreuil
8

Le Durand
10

4

La Petite Bigne
Bn
(4_7)
G

2_4

(6_4)

6_2

4_9

1_2

1_8

1_9

11

(5)

17

Le Benetin

0_3

0_3

0_5

2_4

0_3

0_8

0_6

0_5

Sand

2_r

1_8

5_7

0_7

4_2

4_3

(7_8) G

39
(Old sig. stn)

0_5

8_7

Sand

Statue

Pte de
Rothéneuf

4_5

11

Sand

6_9

7_9

8_8

•17

ROTHENEUF

Windmill

Plan 38   Rothéneuf.

Four miles east of St Malo, this is an extremely tricky place to approach, and it can be a most uncomfortable place to dry out, so it can only be recommended in fine weather and to those experienced in this kind of pilotage.

Approach and Entry

From the E Cardinal Basse aux Chiens buoy, course should be set for La Bigne (approx 230° Mag) until the beacon in the middle of Rothéneuf entrance is bearing about south. Rothéneuf should not be approached with less than 7 metres rise of tide, and at that level the 4·7 m drying rock Le Roger can be ignored. Le Durand, which dries 10 metres near its eastern edge, is usually visible: if it is, steer to leave its most easterly visible part 100 metres to starboard (i.e. pass 100 m east of it) and then for the entrance beacon, which should be left 50 m to starboard, and so into the harbour.

85. Rothéneuf: approach. The entrance beacon is centre: the photograph was taken on the transit with the windmill, but this is hard to pick out.

On the rare occasions when the tide is over 10 metres, and Le Durand is itself invisible, then it is the main danger to avoid, as the south end of Les Hautieux must have more than two metres over it. Approach La Bigne as before, and keep on a straight line from the Basse aux Chiens buoy to the Petite Bigne beacon (keeping north rather than south of the line) until the beacon in the entrance bears 170° True (say 175° Mag), when it may safely be approached on that bearing. The photograph, taken unfortunately in less than ideal visibility, shows the beacon and the general line of approach: the beacon should be left about 50 metres to starboard. If the mill (no sails, but a steeply pitched roof) can be identified, the beacon in line with it gives a safe approach transit, passing 50 m W of le Roger and more than 100 m E of le Durand: it is the most conspicuous house near the skyline in the middle of the bay, just touching the topmark of the beacon in the photograph.

86. The moorings at Rothéneuf. Anchor as close in as possible, but be prepared for some heavy bumps if drying out.

Berthing

There is not much room to anchor on the smooth sandy flats near the village, as most of the space is taken up by moorings, too light for a seagoing yacht. There is room for perhaps two visitors, though, and there are seldom more, but of course the harbour dries, so it is only suitable for bilge-keelers or boats equipped with legs. Even in very calm weather, there was quite enough scend to make the process of drying out and floating off extremely noisy and unpleasant, so I would not really recommend a visit except just for an hour or two around high water: however for those who do decide to stay longer, there is an excellent restaurant and one or two shops in the pleasant little town.

There is a good anchorage outside the harbour entrance, about 250 metres NW of the green entrance beacon, sheltered except from winds with any northerly element. This can be used as a base from which to explore the village at suitable rise of tide; but note that it is a good $\frac{3}{4}$ mile row, so a seaworthy dinghy is needed, and probably a reliable outboard.

Passage Notes: Granville to St Malo

Charts Nos. 3659 and 2700

The best time to leave Granville for St Malo is HW Dover – 3. This is about two hours after HW Granville, so there is still enough water to get out of the harbour, and the fair stream for St Malo is just beginning. The snag is that arrival at St Malo will be around low water, so the visitor will have to wait several hours before he can enter the Bassin Vauban: however Dinard can be reached by most yachts at any state of the tide, and the Bas-Sablons yacht harbour just south of St Malo is available at LW neaps, although at springs one may have to wait until $1\frac{1}{2}$–2 hours after LW.

The passage from St Malo to Granville times much better. The ideal departure is HW Dover + 4 ($3\frac{1}{2}$ hours before HW at St Malo), which gives a fair stream and arrival at Granville around local HW. The first outward locking from the Bassin Vauban in St Malo is not usually until 2 hours before HW St Malo (Dover + $5\frac{1}{2}$), but this still allows three hours of fair or neutral tide, and most yachts will be able to make Granville in time to get in as long as the motor is used if necessary.

The shortest route between the two ports is by the Chenal de la Bigne. Coming from the east, pass north of La Fille N Cardinal buoy (about a mile NE of the light tower on La Pierre de Herpin), and from there steer about west magnetic until the YBY Rochefort beacon tower is identified. Steer for this tower, taking care to avoid getting south of the direct line, until the Basse aux Chiens E Cardinal buoy is identified a mile ESE of the beacon tower. Steer for this buoy, and from a position a cable south of it, a course of 222° True will lead to La Petite Bigne G beacon. The dangerous Le Durand rock is almost always visible, but the part that can be seen should be given a berth of two cables, as a deeper but still dangerous part of the reef extends more than a cable WNW from the highest part of the rock. Leave La Petite Bigne beacon 100 m to starboard, then pass two cables north of the rocks off Pointe de la Varde (the outermost ones do not cover), one cable south of the Letruns and Roches aux Anglais G con buoys, close NE of les Crapauds du Bey buoy (R can) and so SW into the deep water channel. This route carries a least depth of 1·8 metres at MLWS, 4·8 at MLWN. Admiralty chart 2700 or its French equivalent must be carried: it shows a transit for the middle part of the channel, but the marks are a long way off, and this is the safest bit anyway: the approach from Basse aux Chiens buoy to the Petite Bigne beacon is the critical one, and this can be made by keeping the beacon tower on la Crolante (the islet just W of Pte de la Varde) in line with the summit of le Grand Bey, the 23 m high island 400 m W of St Malo. Even this needs pretty good visibility, though, as these marks are difficult for a stranger to pick out when it is misty, but the buoys and beacons are numerous enough to make the channel navigable by anyone experienced in inshore pilotage as long as visibility is at least one mile.

Saint Malo

Charts Nos. 2700, 3659, 2669

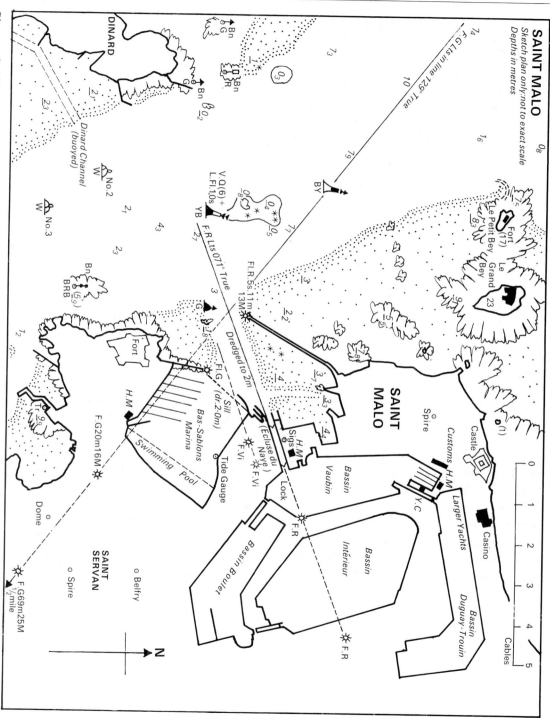

Plan 39   St Malo.

147

Almost totally destroyed during the war, St Malo was rebuilt within its ramparts to its original plan, and it is a charming town with a pleasant and friendly atmosphere.

Approach and Entrance

The approach via the Chenal de la Bigne has already been described. From the north there are the Petits Pointus and Grande Conchée channels, from the NW the main deep water route, the Chenal de la Petite Porte, and from the west the Chenal du Décollé. The last named is very tricky, and should not be attempted on a first visit: the others (all clearly marked on chart 2700) present no problems as long as there is visibility of three or four miles. If arriving near LWS, avoid the Plateau de la Rance, 3 cables W of the north pierhead: at MLWS the rocks have as little as 0·5 metres over them. Entering the outer harbour, keep a good lookout as traffic is heavy. Near LWS there is little room to wait, and it is often worth going into Dinard, whose dredged entrance channel is buoyed and has over 2 m at LWS, for an hour or two.

87. St Malo: the Bas Sablons marina.

148

Berthing (1): Bas-Sablons

The new yacht harbour of Bas-Sablons really attaches to the town of St Servan rather than St Malo. It is protected by a sill 2 metres above chart datum, which therefore has 2·3 metres over it at MLWN, and only dries 0·7 metres at MLWS. The harbour can therefore be entered with average draft at any time during neaps: at springs there is about two metres over the sill two hours before or after low water. The harbour can accommodate boats of up to 20 metres.

All facilities are available including repairs and sailmaker: diesel in cans only. Good shops and restaurants in the little town, about $\frac{1}{2}$ mile from the berths. The dues are among the highest in the area covered by this book: in 1982 they were more than 50% higher than for the Bassin Vauban in St Malo itself (see below).

Berthing (2): Bassin Vauban

This basin (and all the others at St Malo) is entered through a lock, the Ecluse du Naye, just north of the main ferry berth in the Avant Port: it can be hard to identify when closed, especially if there is a large ship in the berth.

88. St Malo: The Bassin Vauban. Harbour office and facilities are in the further left of the two flat-roofed buildings.

The first opening for entry is normally HW $-2\frac{1}{2}$ hours, and the first for exit HW -2 hours: openings continue until about HW $+1\frac{1}{2}$. These times can be affected by the movements of large ships, and one should allow plenty of margin if possible. Once inside, there is a list of times for the next two days posted at the marina office. There are mooring buoys on the north edge of the approach channel: these can be used to wait for an opening, but they dry at LW.

Light signals are displayed at the lock as follows:

R : No entry, departure permitted.

G : No departure, entry permitted.

$\frac{R}{G}$: No entry or departure.

R W or W R: Both gates open: no entry, ships may leave.

G W or W G: Both gates open: no departure, ships may enter.

$\frac{R}{G}$ G : No movement, large ship entering.

$\frac{R R}{G}$: No movement, large ship leaving.

Any other three light signal prohibits movement except to a designated vessel. The lock keeper also has a loud hailer and speaks English, although the combination of accent and distortion can make it a little difficult to understand. There is also a Port Radio, working channel 12.

Once through the lock, yachts turn sharp to port and berth at the north end of the basin, only 150 metres from the centre of town. Boats under 7 m berth W of the W-most pontoon, boats 9-12 m E of the E-most pontoon, the other berths are for 7-10 m overall. Boats over 12 m can berth along the W wall S of the pontoons or, more comfortably, at the W end of the Bassin Duguay-Trouin, W of the numbers 17/16 painted on the wall. To enter this basin a bridge opening has to be arranged either by radio (Ch. 12) or through the harbourmaster.

The town is charming, with excellent shopping and restaurants. There is a Yacht Club overlooking the basin, with bar (open 11-1 and 5-9): sandwiches available. Diesel in cans only (the HM can lend them), but it is a long walk (300 m) and most locals pop in to the quay at Dinard, where one can fill alongside.

Cruising in the Channel Islands

Cruising in this beautiful archipelago needs careful planning, as the rate of tidal stream sometimes encountered can be higher than the maximum speed of the average yacht. Careful study of the tidal stream charts (see pages 124–6) is therefore vitally important, and a constant awareness of the danger of local cross-sets should be cultivated.

Prospective visitors should remember, however, the consoling fact that the charts make the waters look much more dangerous than they really are. This is because of the enormous tidal range, which means that mean level at St Helier, for instance, is 6·1 metres, so that at half tide a reef marked as drying 2 metres will have over four metres of water over it. One can see from this that it is most important when cruising in the area to keep a constant check on the tide level: a Jersey rock drying 10 metres on a day of spring tides will be a pinnacle nearly thirty feet high at LW, while at HW it will be lurking dangerously three or four feet below the surface. But if you know that the tide level at a particular moment is (say) 8 metres, then in reasonable conditions you will know that rocks drying less than five metres can be ignored and those drying more than eight metres are visible, leaving only those between five and eight to worry about. This sort of calculation usually cuts down the problems a lot. In my experience, the Rule of Twelve (the tide rises (or falls) one twelfth of its range in the first hour, two twelfths (one sixth) in the second, three twelfths ($\frac{1}{4}$) in the third and fourth hours, two twelfths in the fifth and one twelfth in the sixth) gives sufficient accuracy for most purposes.

Notes on charts will be found in the Introduction on page 5. Good heavy ground tackle and an ample scope of cable are vital, and remember that the holding in some of the anchorages is only moderate, so always make sure the anchor is holding. I always reverse it in under power, and if it will not hold when the engine is running quarter astern, I haul it up and try again.

A good dinghy is important if the smaller anchorages are to be visited, and shopping should be carefully planned, as some of the harbours in the islands are extremely convenient for the purpose, and others very much the opposite. This is a most interesting and enjoyable cruising ground, despite the requirement for careful and accurate navigation.

Passage Notes: To and from Alderney

Charts Nos. 2669, 3653, 60

The approaches to Alderney from the east present relatively few problems, as long as adequate allowance is made for the very fast streams. Passage Notes Cherbourg to the Channel Islands and West Cotentin (see page 123) explain the westgoing eddy which can help a yacht to reach a position N of Cap de la Hague just as the stream in the Race is beginning to run SW: if bound for Alderney, the Cap should be given a berth of at least two miles, after which it is wise to over-correct for the calculated effect of the stream by 10° or so: once clear N of Quenard Point, any distance wasted will be made up in a matter of minutes. The essential thing is to avoid being carried south and into the Race.

The obvious way south from Braye Harbour, Alderney, is via the Swinge, passing along the N and W coasts of Alderney, but the overfalls and heavy seas that can be encountered when using this route are often far worse than those in the Race itself, and if conditions are doubtful (say SW wind force 4 and a medium tide) it is preferable to work back round Quenard Point and south into the Race. Only heavy and powerful boats should attempt the southbound passage in wind-over-tide conditions with winds above force 4.

If using the Swinge, great care must be taken to avoid the Pierre au Vrai (dr 1·5 m), 2 miles WSW of the W end of Alderney. A white conical beacon just S of Tourgis in line with the N edge of Clonque Rock fort leads safely N of it.

Braye Harbour, Alderney

Charts Nos. 60 and 3653

The only true harbour on Alderney, Braye also has shops and restaurants, although the main town is $\frac{1}{2}$ mile up a steep hill.

Approach and Entry

From the east, the approach is straightforward as long as the shore is given a berth of at least $\frac{1}{2}$ mile. At night, the approach can be along the leading lights: these are difficult to identify in daylight, but then all that is needed is to keep the SE face of the breakwater just barely open and

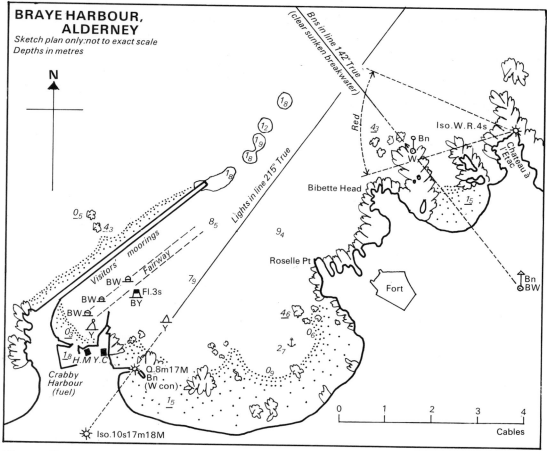

Plan 40   Braye.

153

enter along that line, taking care not to be carried west of the line by the west-going stream. From the west, allowance must be made for the sunken extension of the breakwater near LWS. The shallowest patch, about 2 cables from the pierhead, has 1·2 m at LAT.

Berthing and Facilities

There is now no room to anchor in the western part of the harbour, which is full of moorings, but most of these are for visitors in any case, yachts lying to them two abreast if necessary. One can still anchor in the eastern part of the harbour, and the shelter is much better there in strong NE winds.

Chandlery, and diesel and water alongside can be found in Crabby harbour, the basin at the S end of the western harbour: this dries, and only local boats are allowed to dry there, but there is water for normal draft two hours either side of HW. There is a launch service from the moorings to shore which continues until late enough to dine ashore: 50p per trip per head in 1982. The yacht club has a bar, showers etc., and Braye Guest House, a few yards up the hill towards town, will do baths. There is a splendid restaurant, the First and Last, where the food is not only excellent, but also served by some of the prettiest girls in Europe: advisable to book, ring 3162 or 2535. (Note: the above was a 1982 observation: I can take no responsibility for subsequent staff changes.)

89. Braye Harbour approach: the breakwater (right) must be kept open until clear of the submerged extension.

154

90. Braye: the harbour from up the hill. The anchorage just above the roof at the right of picture is the best place in a NE gale.

There is another small chandler, a hotel and a good shop near the harbour: more extensive shopping, banks etc. in the main town of St Anne, about ½ mile to the south, and some 220 feet above sea level. Braye Harbour operates on channel 12

Other anchorages on Alderney

Some ½ mile SW of Quenard Point is the old harbour of Longy Bay, overlooked by Essex Castle. The entrance is between Raz Island, which has a conspicuous fort, on the east side, and the islet of Queslingue, nearly 50 feet high, on the west. There is a rock which dries over a metre in the middle of the entrance, but this is a drying height above LAT, and at MLWS it has 0·5 m over it, so it is only a problem at springs and near low water. Anchor in 2 m due W of Raz I, and about a cable off the W shore. Exposed in winds between E and S. This is the only really useful anchorage, but La Tchue, another ½ mile to the SW, is a pleasant place to drop the hook for lunch in settled offshore weather: there are fascinating coloured rocks on the northern part of the bay.

Burhou

Chart No. 60

The anchorage at Burhou should only be used during the SW-going tide, but it can be useful for a boat approaching Alderney from the SW by the Swinge and finding itself too late on the tide. The gap between Burhou and Little Burhou must be identified and approached on a course of about 10° True (say 15° Mag.): anchor in the middle of the bay between the two islands in about 4 m. (Note that the gap is spanned by drying rocks, but it is easy enough to distinguish these from 'permanent' land.) This position is right out of the tide, and protected from swell except in strong winds between SE and SW.

Coming from the east, give Noir Homme, the southernmost islet S of Burhou, a berth of 2 cables until on the approach line, and then turn into the anchorage. It will be found that the overfalls of the Swinge can be avoided on the SW stream by keeping well over to the Burhou side: on that side of the channel they do not begin until a cable or so west of the approach line.

Burhou is uninhabited, but there is a cottage that can be hired, and a huge variety of birds nest there.

91. Burhou: just entering the anchorage. Use only on the SW stream.

Passage Notes: Approaches to Guernsey

Chart No. 808

It has already been mentioned that if approaching from the NE against a SW wind, tide-race conditions may be met almost anywhere between Cap de la Hague and Guernsey, and in such conditions it is important to avoid crossing the Banc de la Schole or Alderney S Banks. Coming from this direction, Sark is often sighted some miles before Guernsey is seen, while Herm is indistinguishable from Guernsey until well on in the approach.

The Great Russel channel (between Herm and Sark) is very much clearer and easier than the Little Russel east of Guernsey, and in poor visibility it is often worth using, either cutting across to Guernsey south of the Lower Heads buoy or, if things are very bad, using one of the anchorages on Herm or Sark until the weather improves. In good visibility, however, the Little Russel presents no problems. The Grande Amfroque with its two beacons (BWHS and W) is always easy to identify NE of Herm: from not less than two miles north of this one may steer W, counteracting any southerly set until the Tautenay beacon (BWVS) is bearing 210° True (say 215°M), then steer to pass ½ mile west of it, and then close west of the Roustel beacon if bound for St Peter Port. From the NW, the Grandes Brayes, a mile N of the NE point of Guernsey, may be approached to within ½ mile, from where steer to pass ½ mile east of Platte Fougére beacon (tall and lighthouse shaped, BWHS), and so S for the Roustel. S of Roustel, pass ½ mile W of the unmistakeable squat Brehon tower and so to St Peter Port entrance. South of St Peter Port there are no problems for the careful navigator.

Beaucette Marina

Chart No. 808

Lying near the NE point of Guernsey, the marina is approached from just S of the Petite Canupe buoy, which lies $1\frac{1}{2}$ miles W of Tautenay, and about $\frac{3}{4}$ mile of S of Platte Fougère. Be warned that this unlit S Cardinal buoy is tallish but very skinny and has very small topmarks, so it is quite difficult to spot.

From just S of this buoy the leading line (276° True) can be seen to the W: it consists of a red stripe on the rocks at the N side of the entrance in line with the windsock staff, which also has orange crossbars on it. Keep to this transit: there are R and G channel buoys, but these can float some way off the proper line, especially near LW. The sill in the entrance dries 2·4 metres (tide gauge in entrance) and there is a mooring buoy NE of the entrance on which one may wait for water. The entrance is only 8 m wide at half tide, and should not be attempted in strong winds between N and E. Otherwise the marina can be entered with average draft 2 hours before or after LW neaps, when there will be 1·9 m over the sill: at springs one must be at least $2\frac{1}{2}$ hours from LW, at which time there will be 1·6 m.

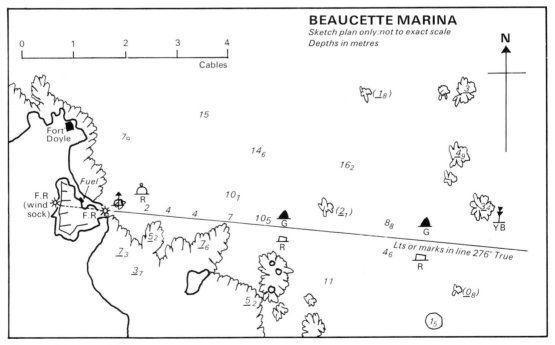

Plan 41   Beaucette Marina.

There is little room for visitors in the marina, but the splendid harbourmaster, Bert Le Noury, will direct and always seems to be able to find another space somehow. If planning a visit in high season, though, it is worth telephoning: the marina number is 45000. There are good showers etc. in the HM building, also a shop selling food and chandlery items, and one of the most celebrated restaurants on the island. It is an interesting and pretty place, an old quarry blasted through to the sea: bear in mind that the water inside is almost bottomlessly deep. The office listens on Channel 16 and Channel M.

92. Beaucette Marina entrance. The rear mark is the windsock staff, above the right of the white HM office: the front one is the red mark framed in white just behind the depth gauge.

St Peter Port

Chart No. 808 and 3140

The main town and harbour on Guernsey, St Peter Port has great character, and recent improvements have made it one of the best and most convenient harbours in the Channel Islands.

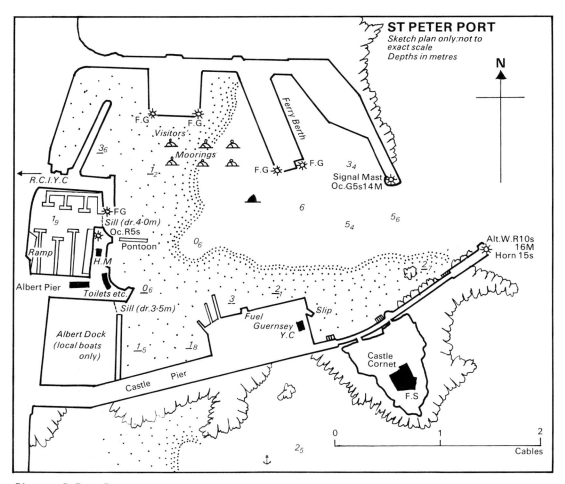

Plan 42 St Peter Port.

Approach and Entrance

The approach has already been covered in the Passage Notes above: the entry is straightforward, but yachts under sail must observe the traffic signals displayed from the N pierhead, a red light prohibiting entry or departure. Yachts (under 18 m) motoring are exempt from this rule, but must keep clear of other traffic. Port Control listens on Channel 16, works channel 12.

Berthing

Yachts are usually met by a harbour control launch, who will direct as to berthing. If not, the Victoria marina, the more northerly of the two basins, is the one used by visitors: visitors' berths are clearly marked. The sill dries 4·0 m, which means that there is some 1·1 m over it at half tide, so for safety most yachts should reckon on being able to get in or out about 2½ hours either side of HW. There is a clear tide gauge in the entrance, and there are mooring buoys in the outer harbour where a boat can lie to await the tide: some of these have very little water at LWS, so take advice if using one on a falling tide. Visitors sometimes have to wait on these buoys for a tide or more in high season, if the marina is completely full.

93. St Peter Port from the NE. The white tower near the left of picture is at the south side of the entrance: the north pierhead, to the right of it, is less conspicuous.

Facilities

St Peter Port is a considerable town, with excellent shops and restaurants etc. only a few minutes from the marina, whose office is on the pierhead south of the entrance. The Royal Channel Islands YC has premises above the Crown pub at the NW corner of the Victoria basin. It opens at 0930 (the bar not until 11.30) and stays open until 2300 with a break from 1430 to 1730. They will keep mail for collection. David Bowker up N Pier Steps is an excellent Class A Chart Agent, also selling navigational equipment, and an Autohelm agent, and there are several chandlers including Marquand Bros, who have been in their premises overlooking the Victoria Basin for 150 years. Further north, opposite the Tourist Bureau, Channel Islands Yacht Services specialise in marine electrics and electronics, and also have engineers. Thorns chandlery on Castle Pier in the outer harbour south side can undertake GRP repairs, and supply fuel. Showers etc. will be found at the seaward end of Albert Pier, beyond the States Housing Authority building: they are open 0700 to 2300 (showers only up to 2200).

St Peter Port is a charming place with an atmosphere all of its own, and well worth a visit.

94. St Peter Port. The marina in Victoria Basin, showing the sill.

Other Ports and Anchorages on Guernsey

(Note: Visitors arriving from outside the Bailiwick should first have cleared Customs at St Peter Port or Beaucette.) Half way between Beaucette and St Peter Port is Guernsey's second harbour, St Sampson. The outer basins dry 3·6 m, the inner ones over 5 m. Local yachts use it quite a lot, but there seems little point in a visitor going there, as it is very commercial and rather dirty. Grande Havre, on the N coast of the island, provides an attractive anchorage sheltered from all but N winds: the approach on a line with the E side of Rousse Point in line with Victoria Tower is not easy for a stranger to identify, but near low water the approach can easily be identified by the offlying Rousse de Mer reef (dr 6·8 m): pass close E of this and then SSE into the bay: a crew member in the bows is advisable. Icart Bay on the S coast offers attractive anchorage in offshore wind, as does Saints Bay, further to the east. The west coast of the island is fringed by a mass of offshore rocks, and yachtsmen are well advised to keep well clear of it.

Numerous transits marking clear passages are marked on chart 808: approaching from the west (say St Peter Port) the easiest is the Alligande Passage. Once the Alligande beacon, $\frac{1}{2}$ mile SE of Brehon, is identified (it has an 'A' topmark) the first transit (Vermerette beacon in line with the end of Herm Pier) is easily seen: once clear of the Epec beacon turn onto 308° True, leaving the Percée rocks to port. The main Herm anchorage is off the west coast of the island, a cable NW of Rosiére steps in about 1 m (i.e. 2 m at LWS), but yachts capable of drying may also find room in the little drying harbour 2 cables further north. It has about 1·5 m at MHWN, 3·8 m at MHWS. The fairway to Rosiére steps must not be obstructed.

95. Herm: the small harbour on the west side of the island.

The other anchorage is on the east side of the island in Belvoir Bay. The approach is relatively straightforward from the south or east, as Noir Pute never covers and can therefore always be used as a landmark. Anchor as close in as the tide allows: the anchorage is exposed to any wind with east in it, and is really only suitable for a picnic stop.

There are a few shops, a hotel, restaurant and pub on the island. Short term anchorage can be found off the east coast of Jethou, a cable N of the beacon on Grande Fauconniére, but the holding is uncertain and the boat should not be left unattended. The jetty at the north of the island is in constant use by commercial launches.

96. The anchorage in Belvoir Bay, Herm.

Sark

Navigation around Sark is easier than it may look at first glance at the chart, as a relatively high proportion of the reefs have islets that never cover, and can therefore always be seen. As anywhere in the Channel Islands, it is important to keep the current height of the tide constantly in mind, to know which rocks are visible, which safely deep, and which lurking dangerously just below the surface; but granted this, the island's waters present problems merely of straightforward pilotage, although a constant lookout must be kept for unexpected cross-sets.

97. Sark. Maseline Harbour from the lighthouse.

Harbours and Anchorages

For the yachtsman there is really no principal harbour: the only enclosed port is Creux, where there is room for four or five boats to dry along the east wall, bilge keels or legs only, bow to anchor. Local advice must be taken to avoid inconveniencing local boats. Just to the north is La Maseline harbour, where perhaps half a dozen yachts have room to anchor inside the line of the jetty. This is sheltered except from E winds, but there always seems to be a good deal of swell and wash, and I have never found it very comfortable. Another $\frac{1}{2}$ mile to the north, La Grève de la Ville is open from N to E, and also suffers from swell. There is a road from Creux and Maseline to the town, which is in the middle of the island, some 100 metres above sea level: the track from La Grève is more suitable for mountain goats.

On the west side of the island, Port la Jument offers a charming anchorage for a picnic, but being totally open to winds from between W and N, I would hesitate to sleep there except in really settled easterly weather. Proceeding south, there is a most exciting passage between Brecqhou and Sark called the Gouliot Passage. This is only 70 metres wide, but deep and clean, and the tide runs through it without undue turbulence when one considers that the rate can

98. Havre Gosselin, Sark. The top left yacht has just passed through the Gouliot Passage, behind the islet at the top centre.

167

exceed ten knots! The southerly stream begins at about 4 hours after HW St Helier, and the northerly about 3 hours before, and one should aim to make the passage during the first or last half hour of the fair tide at springs, or the first or last hour at neaps.

South of the Gouliot one can turn immediately east into Havre Gosselin, where there are a few private moorings, but still room for one or two yachts to anchor. The little bay is well sheltered, but I should think the reflected swell must be pretty severe in SW gales. Stairs and a lane lead to the central town.

Finally, round Little Sark to the southeast coast are perhaps the best, and certainly the most commodious pair of anchorages, Dixcart and Derrible Bays. Both of these offer excellent holding, unlike the other anchorages of the island, and perfect shelter except from between ESE and SSW. Derrible Bay is calmer than Dixcart in westerlies, but the climb up to the upper level of the island is really fierce, whereas that from Dixcart is relatively gentle. Both anchorages are very beautiful, but I must admit a preference for Derrible, rock staircase and all.

All stores are available in the little town, but most people will prefer to pop over to St Peter Port or somewhere else where the walk back to the boat is rather shorter. No facilities of any kind at sea level. Beautiful bathing beaches in the last two bays.

99. The Derrible Bay anchorage, Sark: Dixcart Bay is just the other side of the first headland.

Jersey: Passage Notes, Approaches and Coastal Passages

Chart No. 3655

The majority of British yachts who visit Jersey, the largest of the Channel Islands, do so from Guernsey or Sark, which is convenient, as this involves making landfall on the west coast of the island, which is clear of offlying dangers more than a mile from shore. Rounding Pt Corbière, it is worth noting that when the top of the lighthouse is in line with the high land behind, the boat is 1·7 miles offshore, which is a safe margin. From a position west of Pt Corbière, the inshore passage is easily followed. Steer to pass ½ mile south of Pt de la Moye (a mile east of Corbière light) and from there to pass close south of the light off Noirmont Point, taking care to pass north of the G con buoy (QG) marking the Grande Four rock. Passing close north of another G buoy a mile to the east, one may then continue east until on the St Helier leading line.

This passage can be very rough in wind-over-tide conditions, especially near springs, when the south east coast should be given a berth of at least two miles until St Helier can be approached on a bearing of 023° True.

The north coast of the island is perfectly clear apart from inshore rocks and the two major offshore reefs, the Pierres de Lecq and the Dirouilles, both of which are visible at all times, as they have rocks that never cover. So boats wishing to visit Gorey or St Catherine Bay will often come in on Grosnez Point and then run along the north coast (beware drying rocks extending two cables of Belle Hougue Point) and round to the east coast.

The really tricky passage in Jersey is that between St Helier and Gorey, round the SE corner of the island. The great reef of the Violet Bank dries for more than two miles offshore from La Rocque Point, and other groups of drying rocks are scattered in groups running ESE almost to the French coast. The shortest way round the point is by the Violet Channel, and this presents no navigational difficulties in good visibility, but conditions can be rough enough even in moderate weather to cause difficulties for an average cruising boat in wind-over-tide conditions. Indeed in strong easterlies it may be wiser to time things so as to go the long way round the west and north of the island: a boat leaving St Helier about five hours after HW there will enjoy a mainly fair tide going clockwise round to Gorey. However, neither Gorey nor the St Catherine anchorage are to be recommended in easterlies in any case.

To take the Violet Channel, leave St Helier on the leading line until the Gros du Chateau rocks, conspicuous twin rocks just W of Elizabeth Castle, are in line with the BW mark on the foreshore between St Helier and St Aubin. Once east of the Hinguette buoy (R can, Fl (4) R 15s) steer to pass ½ mile south of the big Demie de Pas beacon (RWVS), and from there steer 110° True for some four miles to the Canger Rock W Cardinal buoy (Q(9) 15s). This is where the true Violet Channel begins, and the worst seas are likely to be met over the next 2–3 miles.

Pass about ¼–½ mile north of the Canger buoy, and alter course to 080° True for the next buoy, RWVS (L Fl 10s). This is usually visible once past the Canger: be sure to keep on the line between them and counteract any cross sets. From the RW buoy (named *Violet*, although this is omitted from some charts) a course of True north will lead into clear water, but be careful not to be set onto the Seal Rocks (dr 1·5 m) 3 cables NW of the Petite Anquette, marked by a beacon. Bound for the French coast, perhaps Portbail or Carteret, pass between the Petite and Grande Anquette beacons and so into clear water.

Proceeding north for Gorey, the outermost rocks off the east coast of Jersey are well marked by beacons and R can buoys, all to be left to port going north.

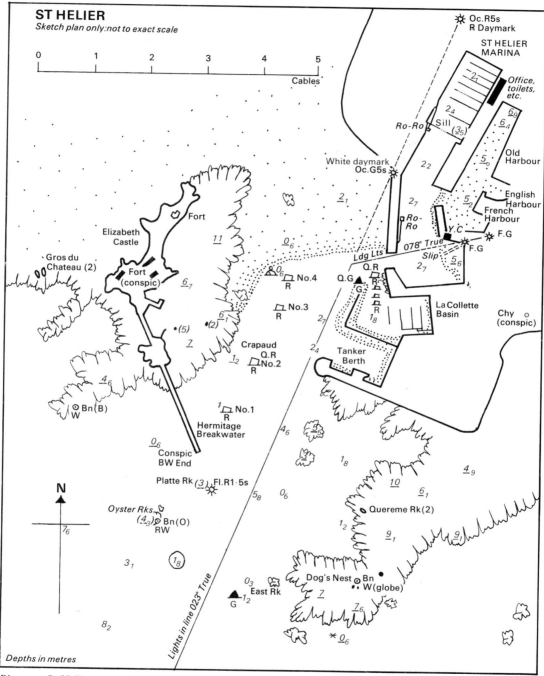

ST HELIER

Sketch plan only: not to exact scale

0   1   2   3   4   5

Cables

Oc.R5s
R Daymark

ST HELIER
MARINA

Office,
toilets,
etc.

Ro-Ro   Sill 2_4 (3_5) 6_9

2_1 6_4

White daymark
Oc.G5s 2_2 5_0 Old
Harbour

2_1 2_7 5_2 English
Harbour

Ro-
Ro   Y.C   French
Harbour

Fort 0_6 Ldg Lts   078° True   F.G

Elizabeth 11 0_6 Slip 5_6 F.G

Castle

Gros du   Fort 6_7 0_6 No.4   Q.R 2_7

Chateau (2)   (conspic)   R   Q.G

6_1 No.3   R   La Collette   Chy
Basin   (conspic)

•(5)   •(2) 2_7 1_8

7 Crapaud   Tanker
Q.R   Berth

1_2 No.2 2_4

R

Bn(B)   No.1 4_6 0_3

W   R 1_8 4_9

Hermitage 6_5 10 6_1

0_6 Breakwater 5_8 0_6 Quereme Rk(2)

Conspic 4_6

BW End 1_2 9_1 9_1

Platte Rk (3) Fl.R1·5s

N   Oyster Rks
(4_3) Bn(O)   Dog's Nest Bn
RW   W(globe)

7_6 3_1 1_8 7 7_6

0_3 East Rk

8_2 1_2 0_6

G

Depths in metres

Lights in line 023° True

Plan 43   St Helier.

The main town and port of Jersey. Yacht facilities have been vastly improved here in recent years, and the harbour now provides comfortable and convenient moorings for visitors at all stages of the tide.

Approach and Entry

The outer approaches have already been dealt with in the general Jersey pilotage section above. From the west, one may steer for the brightly painted end of the Hermitage Breakwater which runs south from Elizabeth Castle until the Oyster Rocks and Platte beacons are identified (the former is a thin RW pole, and not easy to spot). Pass 100 m south of both of these, then steer NNE for the harbour entrance. From the east, pass a cable south of the Demie de Pas RWVS beacon, a cable north of the Hinguette R buoy, and then steer 341° True with Gros du Chateau rock in line with the BW patch on the sea wall between St Helier and St Aubin until on the leading line for the harbour, when it is safe to turn onto 023° True and enter. The leading line is marked by conspicuous W (front) and R (rear) daymarks on Albert Pier, which will easily be seen from this position: at night they are lit, Oc G 5s (front) and Oc R 5s (rear). The harbour

100. St Helier approach. The Hermitage breakwater is on the left.

operates on channels 14 and 82, and yachts with VHF should contact Port Control before entering or leaving. There are traffic signals on the Victoria Pierhead: a G light means that vessels may enter but not leave; R allows departure but not entry; R and G no movement. These signals apply to the main harbour, not La Collette, which is a separate basin to the S, and yachts under power may ignore them but must stay well over to their starboard side and keep clear of commercial traffic.

Berthing (1): La Collette basin

The La Collette basin is available at all times, being dredged to 1.8 m, which is over 3 m at MLWS. The entrance is buoyed: the fairway is only about 25 m wide and looks narrower. It involves a very sharp turn to starboard between the G and R buoys at the entrance, after which the remaining R buoys should be left close to port. On the whole, La Collette is used by yachts waiting for water to proceed into St Helier Marina, as it is a long way from town, though convenient for the yacht club, which is on the elbow of South Pier, where diesel tanks can also be filled, and Calor cylinders replaced. Berthing at La Collette is also indicated if a departure is to be made during the lower half of the tide. Water on the pontoons: toilets near the head of the access ramp.

101. St Helier: the entrance to La Collette yacht harbour: the red buoy must be left to port, which looks most alarming from this angle!

Berthing (2): St Helier Marina

The main marina has a sill drying 3.6 m above Chart Datum, with a gate which closes as the tide falls, rising 1·4 m at the moment when there is 2·2 m over the sill, leaving only 0·8 m. A green light shows when the gate is open, a steady red means it is closed. A flashing red (only shown on a falling tide) means that it is about to close: boats must not attempt to cross against a flashing red unless they are already committed to the final approach. This basin is available 3 hours either side of HW. St Helier Marina, at the N end of the main harbour, is large and modern, with visitors' berths clearly marked. The shops are a couple of hundred yards to the north, but there are showers etc. close to the access ramp. There are several chandlers, and the Channel Islands Yacht Services, who specialise in marine electrics and electronics, have a branch on the north corner of English Harbour, the small basin on the E side of Old Harbour. Excellent shops and restaurants can be found, but take local advice rather than wandering, as St Helier is a rather sprawly town. Don't miss the friendly yacht club (St Helier Y.C.) on Victoria Pier, with a nice bar and a splendid view over the harbour.

Gorey

Charts Nos. 3655 and 1138

Dominated by the magnificent Mont Orgeuil Castle, this drying harbour does not have a great deal of room for visiting yachts, and those that do go inside must be prepared to take the ground.

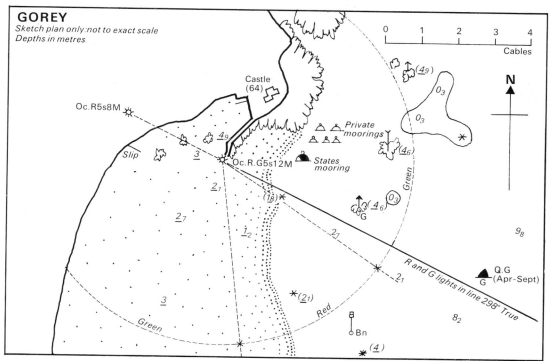

Plan 44   Gorey.

Approach and Entry

The inner harbour dries $3-4\frac{1}{2}$ metres, and so should not be approached below half tide, when there is $3-1\frac{1}{2}$ metres inside. At this level, few of the offshore hazards present any great difficulty, and those that might are marked by beacons, so the pilotage is quite easy. Make the final approach from the G con buoy $\frac{3}{4}$ mile SE of the harbour. At night the leading lights (*rear* Oc R 5s, *front* Oc G 5s on the line, with a R sector beginning just south of the line) give a convenient approach line from the buoy, which is lit QG. Enter round the head of the breakwater and steer north into the harbour.

102. The approaches to Gorey, Jersey, the entrance left centre.

Berthing

Yachts dry on buoys just west of the pierhead, or at the N end near the slip. There is room for a maximum of six boats along the wall, which is the only place where a keel boat can safely dry. There is one mooring buoy outside belonging to the States: it is B conical and normally reserved for commercial ships, but might be available for a yacht by arrangement with the HM: it is in deep water. The other moorings outside the harbour are private.

The harbour operates on Channel 14 VHF. There are showers etc. in the harbour, and diesel can be taken on alongside from Gorey Yacht Services Monday to Friday only: they also do repairs. Enquire at their office by the Dolphin pub at the top of the harbour. The charming little town has shops and restaurants, chandlery etc. It is also a Customs clearing port. The harbour can be uncomfortable or even dangerous in strong winds between east and south.

Other Anchorages in Jersey

Note: None of these anchorages should be used before Customs have been cleared in St Helier or Gorey. Continuing anti-clockwise from Gorey, a popular anchorage is tucked in just south of the great breakwater that extends from Verclut Pt, a mile north of Gorey. Coming from the south, the rocks in the middle of St Catherine Bay must be avoided: there is a beacon on the most easterly part of the reef, but the rocks extend well to the north of the beacon, so care must

176

be taken to keep well E of the beacon until the breakwater is nearly end-on before turning to enter the N part of the bay. Anchor about a cable S of the breakwater, good shelter except in winds from between E and S.

A mile to the NW, Rozel Bay offers anchorage sheltered except in winds from between N and E. There is a tiny fishing harbour where it is occasionally possible to dry (the entrance dries nearly 2 m), or good anchorage outside in W or S winds. Shops, restaurants, bus service to St Helier.

Anchorage can be found on the north coast in Bouley or Bonne Nuit Bays: each has a shop, and the latter has another very small drying harbour. The west coast is exposed to any wind with a westerly component, and would only be used by a yacht as temporary anchorage to shelter from an easterly gale.

On the south coast, St Aubin offers yachts that can take the ground an alternative to St Helier. approaching at half tide or above, make good a course NNW from Diamond Rock buoy for about a mile, when the channel buoys will be seen marking the best water into the harbour. Visitors dry alongside the N quay. The Royal Channel Islands YC has its headquarters here; showers etc. and meals available and a friendly welcome guaranteed. Shops and restaurants in the town, and frequent buses to St Helier some three miles to the east on the other side of the bay.

No visitor to Jersey should leave there without visiting Gerald Durrell's famous zoo at Les Augres Manor, which does such magnificent work in maintaining breeding colonies of endangered species. It can easily be reached by bus from any of the main coastal towns, and a visit makes a memorable outing.

103. Gorey. There is room for just a few yachts to dry along the wall, otherwise they must have legs or bilge keels and dry on a mooring.

The Iles Chausey

Charts Nos. 3656 and 3659

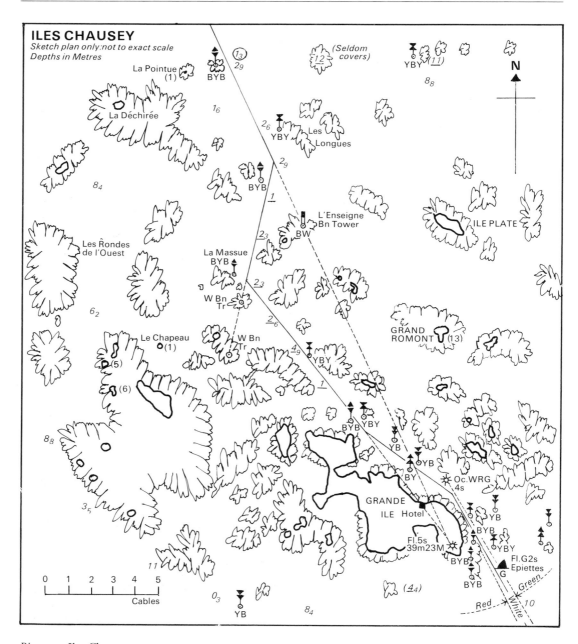

Plan 45   Iles Chausey.

The dedicated rock-hopper can find temporary anchorage under suitable conditions of weather in most of the rock groups in the Channel Islands area, but I do not think there is any place in a general work of this kind for anchorages which can be reached only under limited conditions of wind and tide, and where it would be unwise to sleep without an anchor watch constantly on the alert. The Iles Chausey, on the other hand, offer a charming haven which can be used under most conditions, and which in my opinion deserve to be far better known by British yachtsmen. Of French nationality, the islands lie some ten miles WNW from Granville, and can often provide a valuable staging point as well as being well worth a visit in their own right.

Approach and Entry

The main approach is from the south, and strangers are well advised to make their first entry from that direction even if they are coming from Jersey. In that case the boat should pass close E of the NE Minquiers buoy, and then make good a course of True south until west of Grande Ile, the main island in the group, when course can be altered to pass south of it to the entrance of the haven, which lies on the east side of the island. The rocks extending west of the island are well marked by beacons. The final approach is made from the Epiettes buoy, G conical, Fl G 2s,

104. Iles Chausey: The main lighthouse and the entrance to the harbour.

leaving three E Cardinal beacons to port, and a W and then a N Cardinal to starboard. Then the light beacon is left to starboard (it is a conical structure of iron girders) and course is altered a little to port so as to leave a S Cardinal beacon to starboard and a N Cardinal to port and enter the anchorage. At night, the W sector of the inner sectored light provides a safe line into the anchorage.

The channel which passes right through the rocks and islands from north to south provides an approach from the north at half tide or above, when there is 2 m or so in the shallowest part: I would advise a stranger to explore it for the first time by *leaving* the islands by the northern route. Ideally the large scale French chart (No. 829) should be carried, although it is possible to navigate with British Admiralty 3656 or 3659, the former best if entering the sound from the north, the latter if leaving it from the south. The lighthouse on the southern point of Grande Ile is 39 m high, and can be seen from well north of the northernmost rocks: approach this on 155° True (say 160° Mag.) until the BW Enseigne beacon tower is identified, when this in line with the lighthouse can be used as an approach transit. Coming in on this transit, an E Cardinal beacon will be seen close to starboard, then Les Longues W Cardinal beacon to port. Some 400 metres further on another E Cardinal beacon is left to starboard, and then course is altered to

105. Iles Chausey. Looking south out to sea from the anchorage. The triangular beacon beyond the S Cardinal pole carries the inner sectored light.

193° True (say 198° Mag.) for La Massue beacon. Two white beacon towers provide a transit line for this part of the channel. When La Massue is abeam, a course straight for the lighthouse leads down the remainder of the channel, leaving W Cardinal beacons to port and E Cardinal to starboard. With the large scale chart the pilotage is easy, although a watch must always be kept for cross-sets. Leaving the anchorage and going north through the channel is far easier, as every beacon and transit is approached and identified before it is needed: the lower the tide the better subject to the depths given above, as more of the rocks are visible.

Berthing and Facilities

There are some mooring buoys laid down by the Granville Y.C., and one of these can be picked up if free. Note that many of them dry at LWS. One may also anchor in the channel anywhere north of the jetty used by the ferries. The stream runs north through the sound for the whole of the flood and during the first half of the ebb: it reaches nearly three knots on the flood at springs. The southern entrance has a strong cross tide, and can be very rough in strong southerlies, and the moorings can be very uncomfortable in strong winds blowing up or down the sound, especially near HW. There are two hotels on Grande Ile and one (rather expensive) shop. Visitors should not land on the other islands, most of which are bird sanctuaries with restricted access. This is a most unusual and interesting place with a unique character of its own, and in good weather I think most people will find it well worth a visit.

Appendix: Charts and Books of Reference

Like everything else connected with the sea there is a great deal more to know and learn about chart work than meets the eye on first inspection. Historically it is probable that Gerardus Mercator, some four centuries ago, did more than anybody else to give a chart a modern look. Before him, charts were weird affairs and almost unintelligible to our eyes. Progress is still being made and will continue. Professional seamen keep abreast of these changes and it behoves the yachtsman to do likewise.

The late Dr Peter Pye once remarked that if a man can navigate in the Thames Estuary he can go sailing anywhere in the world—how right he was—and so we have on our own doorstep the most acid of all tests and an ideal training ground.

From this preliminary it is desirable to list some of the changes which are taking place and to enumerate also some of the sources of information.

1.   Since 1968, in order to tie in with the adoption of the metric system, the fathom has been gradually phased out. The new Admiralty charts are now coloured to give clearer indications of shallows and drying areas and almost all now show soundings and heights in metres. Admiralty Tide Tables giving heights and depths in metres were issued from 1972 onwards, and *Reed's Nautical Almanac* gives heights in metres, and metre/feet conversion tables.

2.   Chart datums have now almost all been changed to the level of the Lowest Astronomical Tide (LAT.) These new predicted tidal heights are now incorporated in the Admiralty Tide Tables, Vol. I. When using charts with the old datums MLWS and predicted heights in the new tables, the difference between the two datum levels must be subtracted from the predicted heights.

3.   All yachtsmen should have and study the Mariners' Handbook, published by the Hydrographic Department of the Navy (N.P. 100).

4.   All yachtsmen should have up-to-date charts of their cruising areas and parsimony is not justified in this department, particularly with large scale charts. If, for any reason, old charts are kept and used, then it is advisable to apply to an Admiralty chart agent for Notices to Mariners so that the chart can be maintained up-to-date. These are issued free of charge by the Admiralty, and if they are collected from the chart agents, no charge is made. Most agents are prepared to post them to customers for a small fee to cover postage and packing.

5.   In addition to Admiralty charts, useful charts designed especially for yachtsmen are published by Imray, Laurie, Norie & Wilson, and Stanford Maritime.

6.   Tidal Stream information can be obtained from the diagrams in *Reed's Nautical Almanac*, which are smaller scale reproductions of the Admiralty Pocket Tidal Stream Atlases for the Straits of Dover and the English Channel. The originals, being larger, are easier to use, but best of all is Stanford's Tidal Atlas (English Channel East), which is on a still larger scale. This is available from the publishers, Stanford Maritime, 12–14 Long Acre, London WC2 (Tel. 01-836 1321).

7.   The *Cruising Association Handbook* and the Admiralty *Channel Pilot* also contain much helpful information.

8.   French government charts are obtainable to order from J. D. Potter Ltd., of 145 The Minories, London EC3 (Tel. 01-709 9076).

9.   There are also special coloured yachtsmens' charts produced in France by Editions Cartographique Maritime. They are called Cartes-Guide Navigation Cotiére, and provide a mass of ancillary detail. From Calais to Cherbourg, the numbers required are 1010, 1011, 1012, 526, 527 and 528. They are produced on rather thin paper, and so not very suitable for use in an exposed cockpit, but the information they contain on tides, prevailing winds etc., can be helpful when planning a cruise, or the next day's passage. These are inconspicuously dated in small figures on the lower right hand corner of the back cover; be sure that you buy up-to-date editions. Available at J.D. Potter Ltd.

10.   Finally, for readers wishing to go up the Seine, the best map easily available in England is the Carte de Navigation Fluviale, *Paris à la Mer par le Canal de Tancarville*, available at Potters. This covers the passage from Le Havre to Paris by way of the Tancarville canal: the lower Seine from Honfleur to Tancarville presents no difficulties. However, if only going as far as Rouen, ample coverage appears on Carte Guide No. 1012.